TABLE OF CONTENTS

Top 20 Test Taking Tips

1. Carefully follow all the test registration procedures

2. Know the test directions, duration, topics, question types, how many questions

3. Setup a flexible study schedule at least 3-4 weeks before test day

4. Study during the time of day you are most alert, relaxed, and stress free

5. Maximize your learning style; visual learner use visual study aids, auditory learner use auditory study aids

6. Focus on your weakest knowledge base

7. Find a study partner to review with and help clarify questions

8. Practice, practice, practice

9. Get a good night's sleep; don't try to cram the night before the test

10. Eat a well balanced meal

11. Know the exact physical location of the testing site; drive the route to the site prior to test day

12. Bring a set of ear plugs; the testing center could be noisy

13. Wear comfortable, loose fitting, layered clothing to the testing center; prepare for it to be either cold or hot during the test

14. Bring at least 2 current forms of ID to the testing center

15. Arrive to the test early; be prepared to wait and be patient

16. Eliminate the obviously wrong answer choices, then guess the first remaining choice

17. Pace yourself; don't rush, but keep working and move on if you get stuck

18. Maintain a positive attitude even if the test is going poorly

19. Keep your first answer unless you are positive it is wrong

20. Check your work, don't make a careless mistake

Human Development and Behavior

Psychoanalytic Theory

Psychoanalytic theory postulates that behavior is influenced not only by environmental stimuli (physical influences) and external social constraints and constructs (taboos, mores, and laws, as well as conduct deemed praiseworthy and honorable), but by four specific unconscious elements as well. According to psychoanalytic theory, the four elements of the unconscious mind that shape behavior are: covert "desires,""defenses" needed to protect, facilitate, and moderate behaviors, "dreams," and unconscious "wishes."

Because these elements exist only in the unconscious mind, individuals remain substantially unaware of all the forces, motivations, and drive which shape their thoughts and behavioral decisions.

Psychoanalysis Primary Focus

The primary focus of psychoanalysis is on the unconscious mind and the desires, defenses, dreams, and wishes contained therein. Freud proposed that the key features of the unconscious mind arise from experiences in the past and from problems in the development of the personality. Consequently, a focus on the unconscious mind requires the psychoanalytic process to also focus on the past—specifically on those repressed infant and childhood memories and experiences which served to create the desires, defenses, dreams, and wishes that invariably become manifest through the thoughts and behaviors of every individual.

Freud's Theory

Freud's psychoanalytic theory suggests that all thoughts and behaviors are driven by various forces and motives within the mind and always serve some underlying purpose, whether one is aware of the purpose or not. Freud proposed three levels of the mind. They are: The three levels of the mind proposed by Freud are:

- The "conscious" mind, comprising various ideas and thoughts of which we are fully aware.
- The "preconscious" mind, comprising ideas and thoughts outside of immediate awareness but which can be readily accessed and brought into awareness.
- The "unconscious" mind, comprising thoughts and ideas outside of our awareness and which cannot be accessed or brought into full awareness by personal effort alone.

Personality Structural Theory

Freud proposed a three-level structure of personality, composed of the id, the ego, and the super-ego. The id is that level of personality comprising basic instinctual drives (including the sexual drive called the "libido") and is the only portion of personality present at birth. The id seeks immediate gratification of primitive needs (hunger, thirst, reproduction) and adheres to the "pleasure principle" (seek pleasure, avoid pain). The ego develops secondarily and allows for rational thought, executive functions, and the ability to delay gratification. The ego is governed by the "reality principle" and mediates between the desires of the id and the requirements of the external world. The super-ego develops last and incorporates the higher concepts of morality, ethics, and justice into the personality, allowing concepts of right, wrong, and greater good to override base instincts and purely rational goals.

Executive Function

Executive functions are those cognitive features that control and regulate all other abilities and behaviors. Executive functions are higher-level abilities that influence attention, memory, and motor skills. Executive functions also monitor actions and provide the capacity to initiate, stop, or change behaviors, to set goals and plan future behavior, and to solve problems when faced with complex tasks and situations. Executive functions allow us to form concepts and think abstractly. Deficits are evident in the reduced ability to delay gratification, problems understanding cause and effect (i.e., concrete thinking), poor organization and planning, difficulty following multi-step directions, perseveration with an idea in the face of superior information, and overall poor judgment.

The Super-Ego

The super-ego comprises the "conscience" and the "ego ideal"—constructed from the restraints and encouragements provided by caregivers (parents, teachers, and other guiding members of society). The conscience focuses on cognitive and behavioral restrictions (the "should nots"), while the ego ideal focuses on perfection, including spiritual attainment and higher-order goals (the "shoulds" of thought and behavior). Thus, the super-ego works in opposition to the id, producing feelings of guilt for inappropriate drives, fantasies, and actions and encouraging refinement, aspirations, and higher-order goals. Freud postulated that this last aspect of the personality emerges around age five. In a healthy person, the super-ego is not the dominant feature of the personality, as this would result in overly rigid, rule-bound behavior. Rather, the ego is the strongest, in order to satisfy the needs of the id without disrupting the superego, as rationally moderated by the reality of every situation.

Reciprocal Exchange

Freud believed that an individual's mental state emerged from the process of reciprocal exchange between two forces: "cathexis" and "anti-cathexis." While Freud used the term *cathexis* to refer to the psychic energy attached to an object of importance (e.g., a person, body part, psychic element), he also used it to refer to "urges" (psychic impulses such as desires, wishes, pain, etc.) that drive human behavior. In contrast to the driving urges of cathexis, there is a "checking force" he called anti-cathexis. It serves to restrict the urges of the id, and also serves to keep repressed information in the unconscious mind.

Personality Development

Freud identified two primary elements that contribute to the development of the personality:
natural growth and maturational processes (biological, hormonal, time-dependent processes) and learning and experiential processes (coping with and avoiding pain, managing frustration, reducing anxiety, and resolving conflicts).

Healthy development depends upon successfully progressing though five developmental stages:
the oral stage, the anal stage, the phallic stage, the latency stage, and the genital stage.
Psychopathology will result if all stages of development are not fully mastered, or if fixation at a particular stage develops (resulting if needs at a particular stage are either under- or over-gratified). If significant developmental frustration is experienced in a later stage, the developmental process may fall back to an earlier stage by means of the defense mechanism known as regression.

Psychosexual Development

The first stage of psychosexual development is called the "oral" stage. It comprises the period between birth and about 18 months of age. As its name indicates, this is the period when gratification is derived from oral stimuli (e.g., nourishment and sensations such as taste and texture). The "anal" stage follows, from about 18 to 36 months of age. Here the individual's focus shifts from oral preoccupation to anal preoccupation and the elimination of bodily wastes. Sphincter control is established. The "phallic" stage comprises ages 3–6 years, as the focus moves to genital awareness. The "latency" stage occurs from ages 6 to 12 years and is where genital preoccupation takes on social constraints and mores. The "genital" stage comprises ages 12 to adulthood and is characterized by genital acceptance, maturation, and adult-oriented sexual feelings.

The "Oedipus complex" arises for male children during the phallic stage. It is characterized by jealousy of the father and competition for the mother's attention and affection. Conflict occurs through fear of castration by the father (Freud's "Castration" theory) in retaliation. Development of the super-ego aids in concluding the phallic stage, allowing resolution of the Oedipus complex and a return to identification with an emulation of the father's values and beliefs. The "Electra complex" occurs with female children between the ages of 3 and 7 years and is evident in a girl's sexual attraction to her father. Key characteristics include an awareness of the lack of male genitalia and blaming the mother for this deficit. Super-ego development and maturation resolves the complex.

Defense Mechanisms

Anna Freud proposed the concept of "defense mechanisms." She postulated that they serve to protect the ego and to reduce angst, fear, and distress through irrational distortion, denial, and/or obscuring reality. Defense mechanisms are deployed when the ego senses the threat of harm from thoughts or acts incongruent with rational behavior or conduct demanded by the super-ego. "Acting out" involves performing an action in place of direct coping with feelings (e.g., breaking something instead of talking out anger). "Avoidance" is a refusal to encounter something because of unconscious impulses (aggression, etc.) and/or as punishment for those impulses.

Compartmentalization" involves separating certain parts of the self from awareness of other parts to avoid the "cognitive dissonance" (guilt) of behaving in opposition to one's own values.

"Compensation" involves counterbalancing perceived weaknesses by emphasizing other strengths—for example, the exercise of power to compensate for other perceived deficits (e.g., the "Napoleonic complex," where angst over short stature is compensated by increased aggression). "Denial" involves a refusal to recognize or accept reality to avoid the associated discomfort, pain, and/or anxiety that would otherwise accompany the recognition or acceptance. "Displacement" involves a shift of repressed feelings from the actual source to other people or objects that are less threatening. "Dissociation" occurs when feelings accompanying an experience, situation, or thought are entirely separated or at least temporarily set aside. "Fantasy" is the use of internal imagery as a method of coping, such as fantasizing about success to ward off feelings of failure. "Idealization" occurs when desirable qualities are overemphasized to cope with/mask the limitations of a desired object, as when a purchaser expounds the virtues of an already chosen item when confronted with an alternative.

The defense mechanism of "identification" is seen when someone unconsciously models the desirable behaviors, beliefs, and/or roles of another. "Introjection" involves identification to the extent that one fully internalizes the ideas, behaviors, or attributes of another person or object. "Inversion" occurs when emotions, such as aggression, that arise from an external source are turned inward toward oneself.

"Isolation" refers to splitting away the emotions normally accompanying a thought or experience (e.g., when a bank teller remains calm during a robbery but is tearful and tremulous afterward). "Intellectualization" involves a cognitive focus to the exclusion of emotions in order to cope with potentially overwhelming circumstances (e.g., focusing on the processes of treatment rather than the import of receiving a life-threatening diagnosis). "Projection" refers to the assignment of one's undesired impulses to another (e.g., an angry person accuses another of hostility).

"Rationalization" involves the use of distorted, faulty, or incomplete logic to justify a desired outcome, impulse, or action. "Reaction formation" refers to overcompensation for unacceptable impulses, such as leading a campaign against a desired vice, or a married woman treating one of her husband's friends rudely because of a hidden attraction. "Regression" is reverting to a lower level of development or adaptation in the face of overwhelming stress, threat, or anxiety. "Repression" refers to the exclusion of a painful or conflicted thought, impulse, or memory from awareness. "Resistance" is evident as a deep-seated opposition to allowing any awareness of repressed (unconscious) anxiety-provoking thoughts, memories, experiences, or information to awareness. "Somatization" is the emergence or production of physical symptoms from emotional distress or anxiety.

"Splitting" involves characterizing people, situations, etc., as "all bad" or "all good" to reduce the need to cope with negative aspects (any evidence to the contrary is ignored, repressed, dissociated, etc.). "Sublimation" occurs when unacceptable impulses are converted into some other more acceptable form (e.g., taking up boxing to relieve one's pent-up frustration or need for violence). "Substitution" involves unconsciously replacing an unattainable or unacceptable goal, emotion, or object with one that is more attainable or acceptable (e.g., unconsciously deciding to be a paralegal because the prospect of becoming an attorney is too stressful). "Undoing" refers to the attempt to retrieve or recover behaviors, thoughts, or expressions that are unacceptable after they have been acted out, thought, or verbalized. An example of undoing would be expressing excessive praise for someone after having insulted that person.

Heinz Hartmann's Ego Psychology

Ego psychology was derived from psychoanalytic theory and focuses on the ego in Freud's theory of personality. Central tenets include: everyone is born with the capacity to adapt to social environments, as both the id and the ego are present at birth (contrary to Freud's belief that only the id is present at birth), the ego is primarily responsible for adaptation. adaptation requires ego-based choices; and adaptation occurs via: "alloplastic behavior" (adaptive changes to the environment) or "autoplastic behavior" (adaptive changes to the self).

Successful adaptation is accomplished by way of 12 major ego functions, which facilitate the change and adaptation process in social environments. Hartmann's twelve ego functions include:

- reality sensation, the capacity to both perceive and experience things in the environment accurately
- reality testing, which refers to the capacity to differentiate and make accurate observations regarding the self and the environment
- judgment, the capacity to identify a behavior and successfully weigh the consequences of carrying it out prior to taking any action
- drive and impulse control, the capacity to regulate drives and impulses in concert with reality
- object relations, the capacity to relate to and interact with others
- controlled thought processes, the capacity to organize and direct thoughts toward realistic ends and goals
- adaptive regression, the capacity to suspend reality in order to experience portions of the self that would not otherwise be accessible

- defensive functioning, the capacity to reduce anxiety and mitigate otherwise painful experiences by means of unconscious self-preservation mechanisms
- stimulus barrier, the capacity to accommodate increases and decreases in environment stimulation sufficient to maintain the current level of functioning
- autonomous functions, the capacity for essential conflict-free functions to occur independently and concurrently, such as concentration, learning, memory, and perception
- mastery-competence, the capacity to engage the environment successfully; and
- integrative functioning, the capacity to resolve conflict by integrating certain parts of the personality.

Margaret Mahler's Object Relations Theory

Margaret Mahler's object relations theory is another offshoot of psychoanalytic theory. The emphasis is on interpersonal relationships, particularly between mother and child. An "object" is something to which one relates—usually persons, parts of persons, or symbols of one of these.

Key concepts include: the drive to understand the self and others is present from birth; the drive to build interpersonal relationships is present at birth; all interpersonal relationships are affected by the quality of an individual's understanding of self and others; residues of past relations affect a person in the present; during the first 3½ years of life, a child learns to differentiate between the self and others; and object relations arise through a child's ego organization during the first 3½ years of life.

Mahler's three stages of development are:
- the "autistic" stage (newborn to 1 month), in which total focus on self and oblivious to external stimuli.

- the "symbiotic" stage (1–5 months after birth), in which the "need satisfying object" (the mother) begins to be identified as such and, gradually, as separate from the self.

- the "separation-individuation" stage (5 months to 2 years and beyond), which consists of four substages: differentiation (5–9 months), the shift to an outward focus, and early separation from the caregiver; practicing (9–14 months), in which autonomous ego functions begin to emerge, along with increasing mobility; rapprochement (14–24 months), in which is the move away from the mother, but with regular returns; object constancy (after 24 months), in which the mother relationship becomes internalized, with the child recognizing her continued existence even when she is absent.

Heinz Kohut's Self-Psychology

Psychoanalytic self-psychology rejects Freud's primary focus on the sexual drives in the organization of the human psyche, as instinctual drives are not seen as integral to the development of a cohesive self. The role of empathy is seen as crucial in human development, with nurturing "selfobjects" seen as paramount (as people and objects are perceived by the infant as part of the self). The primary selfobject (the mother) attends to the child by way of "empathic mirroring" (hearing and responding to the child's needs), which ultimately helps the child to develop a cohesive self-identity. Thus, self-psychology sees the self/selfobject relationship as the primary focus, as opposed to the self-object relationship of object relations theory. The cohesive self is attained through "transmuting internalization," by which positive, healthy objects are incorporated into the self-structure. Kohut saw narcissism as a normal and integral part of development. Abnormal narcissism occurs only when an empathic environment is lacking, leaving the child unable to transform early grandiose self-images into a more realistic self.

Fritz Perls' Gestalt Psychology

As suggested by the name *Gestalt* (a derivative of the German word for "wholeness"), this theoretical approach focuses the individual from a holistic perspective. Although Gestalt theory recognizes the role of unconscious drives, it opts to focus primarily on the "here and now" rather than the influences of the past. Even so, many issues and problems are seen as rooted in past experiences (both relational and environmental). However, immediate behaviors are perceived as fully conscious choices that are entirely in the individual's control, along with the power to change. This theory does not subscribe to any discrete, multi-stage process of personal development, which is instead seen as a process unique to each individual. Rather than focusing on personality as an aggregation of parts, it is seen as parts integrated into a whole.

Erik Erikson's Psychosocial Theory

Erikson's psychosocial theory has roots in psychoanalytic theory but incorporates key elements form Hartmann's ego psychology. Primarily, psychosocial theory concurs with a less deterministic view of the personality, as compared with the psychoanalytic view, and thus emphasizes the capacity for personality growth and change. Even so, views of individual functioning are still guided by the psychoanalytic model. As with ego psychology, the ego is seen as the most important part of the personality (e.g., id, ego, and super-ego). While Erikson accepts Freud's belief that childhood experiences shape much of a personality, he felt that personality development continued past the age of 5. The foundation of psychosocial theory is that all individuals have innate value and the capacity to learn and adapt and to influence their environment (both socially and physically). Biological and social system influences are acknowledged, though the psychosocial system is seen as paramount in determining behavior.

Erikson was one of the first theorists to address human development over the entire life span. Psychosocial theory proposes eight developmental stages:

- trust vs. mistrust
- autonomy vs. shame
- initiative vs. guilt
- industry vs. inferiority
- identity vs. role confusion
- intimacy vs. isolation
- generativity vs. stagnation
- ego integrity vs. despair

The stages are hierarchical, building upon each other, and resolution of the fundamental "crisis" of each prior stage must occur before one can move on to the next stage of growth. Stages are a compound of two opposing personality features referred to as "syntonic" and "dystonic"—where proper development requires achieving a balance between the two, but tending toward the syntonic. Although individual attributes are primary in resolving the crisis associated with each stage, the social environment can play an important role as well.

The first of Erikson's stages of psychosocial development is "trust vs. mistrust," which unfolds from birth to 1 year of age. During this stage, a child should develop a strong sense of trust, due to the nurture and love that is shown. Where affectional and nurturing elements are absent, mistrust can result and manifest itself as emotional withdrawal in later life. The second stage is "autonomy vs. shame and doubt," which unfolds between 2 and 3 years of age. During this time, increasing motor and verbal skills precipitate greater confidence and control, allowing a child to develop a rudimentary sense of autonomy. Lacking social nurturance, confidence is eroded and shame and doubt may emerge. The third stage is "initiative vs. guilt," which is experienced between 4 and 5 years of age. Burgeoning physical and cognitive capacity leads to curiosity and exploration. Active play with others is an

- 16 -

important feature of this period. Where initiative (curiosity, exploration, and play) is not allowed, guilt and fear may result. The fourth of Erikson's psychosocial stages of development is "industry vs. inferiority." This developmental stage is experienced between 6 and 11 years of age. During this stage a child must develop mastery over tasks and activities in key areas such as school and peer and family relationships. If a sense of adequate mastery is lacking in each of these domains, feelings of inferiority and incompetence may emerge. The resulting sense of failure can significantly handicap the developmental process and the individual's future life course. The fifth stage is "identity vs. role confusion," which unfolds between 12 and 18 years of age (e.g., during the period of adolescence). During this period, a person seeks to establish a unique self-identity and to integrate the developing parts of the self into an authentic and whole individual.

The sixth of Erikson's psychosocial stages of development is "intimacy vs. isolation," which unfolds between 20 and 35 years of age. This period is characterized by relationship building in social, occupational, and sexual areas. Each of these relationships comprises a significant area of personal development, essential to holistic success in life. Failure in building responsive and functional relationships can lead to feelings of isolation and estrangement. The seventh stage is "generativity vs. stagnation," which unfolds between 35 and 50 years of age. During this stage, individuals refine the capacity to care, nurture, and sustain others. Individuals who fail to resolve this stage may become increasingly narcissistic and self-occupied. The final developmental stage is "ego integrity vs. despair," which encompasses the period of life beyond 50 years of age. This period is significant for the acceptance of personal achievements and life setbacks and the accomplishments of others. Failing to reconcile this stage can result in feelings of despair.

Normal Physiological Development

The newborn period is characterized by sensory and reflexive development—vision, oral sensation, the sucking reflex, etc. Physiological features during the first month of life include increased muscle strength and reflex development in the extremities (arms and legs). During the second month of life, reaching and holding is improved, efforts are made at holding up the chin, and hair growth is more apparent. By the third month, an infant can hold up the chest while lying in a prone position (on the stomach). During the fourth month teething begins, and rotation of the head can be accomplished in all directions. The fifth month finds improved eye–hand coordination and the capacity to move by rolling and rocking. Between the sixth and eighth month of life, balance improves, leading to sitting up with some help and crawling.

From 9 to 12 months of age, a child learns to stand alone, begins to walk, and can climb up stairs with help. Between 15 and 17 months, a child begins to walk unaided, learns to throw objects, and develops the capacity to walk sideways and backward. Between 18 and 19 months of age, a child refines grasp-and-release maneuvers and develops the ability to run and to jump with both feet. Language begins to develop, and several simple words and short phrases are known. At the 2 years, a child has a repertoire of 50 or more words and can form two-word sentences. Bladder control is also evident. Between 3 and 4 years of age, a child begins to dress independently and can draw circles and scribble. By age 6 a child can learn to print and read his or her own name, and permanent teeth begin coming in.

Between 7 and 11 years of age, there is a significant divergence in motor skills between the genders. From 12 to 15 years of age (pubescence), motor coordination improves. From 16 to 18 years of age, the sex organs mature, growth (in both height and weight) is slower, and muscle mass increases. Between the ages of 18 to 30, adult size is attained. Between ages 30 to 35, height begins to decrease and body fat begins to increase. From 35 to 60 years of age, vision and hearing steadily decline, hair loss may occur, reaction times are reduced, gross motor skills decrease, and (on average) between 45 and 55 years of age, menopause occurs in women. From ages 60 to 70, hair loss accelerates and tooth loss may begin. Decreases in muscle tone and height continue, and sensorimotor deficits become more apparent. From age 70 onward, muscle and bone deterioration accelerates, along with greater hearing and vision loss, and coordination becomes poorer. The body becomes more vulnerable to indices of mortality.

Development Theories

Jean Piaget

Piaget proposed that all human development and behavior arises from interactive patterns or templates called "schemas." Schemas are the cognitive constructs through which one explores and learns about the physical and social world. Schemas are goal-oriented systems of mental organization that are both sensorimotor (movement and sensory based) and cognitive (perception and experience based). Learning occurs via "adaptation," a two-part process consisting of: "*assimilation*" (integration of perceptions into a schema) and "*accommodation*" (modifying a schema to fit a new object, experience, or situation).

Piaget believed that a child's processes of cognitive development can be categorized into four hierarchical stages: sensorimotor, preoperational, concrete operational, and formal operational.

The "sensorimotor" stage extends from birth to 2 years of age. During this stage, an infant explores the world using motor functions and sensoria—the sucking reflex plays a prominent role (e.g., nursing). Early circular interactive patterns emerge (e.g., thumb-sucking is pleasant, which then reinforces the behavior). During this stage, the infant is unable to utilize symbolic representation—i.e., he/she cannot relate to objects or people when they are absent. The "preoperational" stage extends from 2 to 7 years of age. During this period, the child develops the capacity for symbolism, evident in drawing, language, and speech. The child becomes increasingly cognizant of the concepts of a past and a future (e.g., a crying child can be comforted with assurances such as "We'll be going home soon"). A self-centered focus predominates during this period ("It's all about me").

The "concrete operational" stage encompasses the ages between 7 and 11 years. During this stage a child develops the capacity to manipulate symbols in a logical fashion. For example, whether you stack two items or place them in a row, the child will still indicate that there are only two items involved. During this period a child will also come to understand the principle of "conservation of substance." Thus, when punch is poured from a pitcher into four glasses, the child will still understand that the total amount of punch involved remains the same. The final stage is the "formal operational" stage, which extends from age 11 to age 15 years. During this stage, a child is able to begin cognitively perceiving and analyzing his or her world in adult ways. Logical operations move from being solely concrete in nature to encompass abstract thinking. Consequently, the concept of "hypothetical thinking" (also called "abstract thinking") is developed during this stage.

Alfred Adler's and Albert Ellis' Cognitive Theories

Adler is the founder of "individual psychology" (more correctly translated as "indivisible psychology," requiring a holistic approach). This cognitive approach incorporates psychodynamic, cognitive-behavioral, existential, and humanistic principles. It differs from Freud's psychoanalytic approach in three key ways: the personality is not subdivided but must be viewed as a whole; social motivation (not sexual drive) guides behavior; and conscious thoughts and beliefs are paramount (as opposed to Freud's focus on the unconscious)—although unconscious misconceptions, false beliefs, and irrational thoughts do exert influence. Physiological, neurological, and chemical problems can also shape behavior.

Ellis founded the cognitive theory known as Rational Emotive Therapy (RET), also referred to as the "ABC theory of emotion." The theory holds that rational thought produces psychological health. Using the ABC model, the "A" refers to any activating event; "B" refers to beliefs about "A"; and "C" refers to the consequences (emotional and behavioral). Rational thought ensures functional beliefs and successful consequences.

Lawrence Kohlberg's Moral Development Theory

Kohlberg created his theory to extend and modify Piaget, as he believed that moral development was a longer and more complex process. He postulated that infants possess no morals or ethics at birth and that moral development occurs largely independently of age. He suggested a process involving three levels, each with two stages. The first is the "preconventional level." Stage 1 is engaged around school age (birth to 9 years) and involves adherence to social norms to escape punishment. Stage 2 adds personal "best interests," where possible. The second level, the "conventional level" (ages 9–15) includes Stage 3, which is characterized by "approval seeking," and Stage 4, which incorporates an awareness of laws and rules. Finally, the "postconventional level" (ages 15 to adult) is ushered in with Stage 5, wherein an individual looks outside him/herself to comprehend social mutuality. Stage 6 is entered when one shapes behavior by individual conscience. Kohlberg felt that few people fully attain the final level, with, perhaps, no one having ever entirely engaged Stage 6.

Behavioral and Social Learning Theories

Behavioral theory postulates that all behaviors are learned, in one way or another, and thus all behaviors can be "unlearned" or changed. The two fundamental theories supporting behavioral theory are: *classical* (or respondent) conditioning, the way in which behavior is learned and reinforced by a process of positive association; and *operant conditioning*, the way in which behaviors are learned by way of positive or negative reinforcement. Social learning theory also postulates that all behaviors are learned but focuses on altering the events before and after a target behavior to bring about change. The earliest theorists responsible for formulating classical conditioning were John Watson and Ivan Pavlov, while operant conditioning was developed by B. F. Skinner. A primary proponent of social learning theory was Albert Bandura.

Social Learning Theory

Social learning theory has three specific components that are used to shape behavior: 1.) an "antecedent event" (some environmental event which arises before the target behavior), 2.) the "target behavior" (the act to be changed), and 3.) the "consequence" (an outcome of the behavior). Manipulation of 1.) and/or 3.) will result in altered behavior (e.g., ignoring rather than reacting to a tantrum) and will eventually extinguish it).

Conditioning

Classical Conditioning

Classical (or "respondent") conditioning produces behavior by means of association, such as pairing a positive stimulus with a neutral stimulus to produce a behavior. The behavior elicited (a "conditioned response") can be either "emitted" (voluntary) or "reflexive" (involuntary). Ivan Pavlov demonstrated this with his famous study of dog salivation, wherein food was presented to dogs with the ringing of a bell. Food was the "unconditioned stimulus" (US), and salivation at seeing food was the "unconditioned response" (UR). Eventually the dogs salivated at the sound of the bell absent any food. Thus, the bell became the "conditioned stimulus" (CS), and salivation became the "conditioned response" (CR). Similarly, John B. Watson was famous for his "Little Albert" experiment, which produced a conditioned response in a child. Given a rabbit to play with, Watson would produce a loud clanging noise behind the child whenever he engaged the rabbit. Eventually the child became terrified at the sight of the rabbit.

Operant Conditioning

Operant conditioning involves changes in the environment coupled with reinforcement by significant others, resulting in behavioral change. "Reinforcement" is the process by which positive or negative stimuli result in increased or decreased behavior. Positive reinforcement can be any of a variety of rewards (praise, treats, privileges, etc). Negative reinforcement uses aversive events or items (anything undesirable) which will cause a specific behavior to avoid or escape the negative reinforcer. Punishment is not the same as negative reinforcement. Negative reinforcement is used to increase a target behavior, while punishment is designed to decrease a target behavior.

Issues of Diversity

Cultural Competence

Cultural competence is the faculty of being able to respond to all socioeconomic classes, cultures, languages, races, and religions with appropriate attitudes, behaviors, and policies to work effectively in cross-cultural situations. This requires sensitivity to a client's age, culture, gender, race, religion, and sexual orientation. A culturally competent practitioner must gain awareness and knowledge about cultural differences; know his/her own personal beliefs, culture, and values; understand the dynamics of differences and ethnocentricity; know how to express his/her limits of cultural understanding; pursue insights into the meanings of economic status, family, and religion, as well as varying levels of acculturation and the prevalence of culture-bound syndromes. Organizations must develop a diverse staff, implement culture-sensitive policies, and require employee cultural self-assessments. Issues of abuse indigenous to cultures, however, must be assessed in the context of American standards and laws, albeit with awareness of and sensitivity to barriers in language, affect, behavior, trust, and response patterns.

Prejudice and Discrimination

Prejudice refers to "pre-judging" based upon personal values, negative inferences, and normative judgments. Discrimination is prejudice expressed or implied; the withholding of choices, benefits, or opportunities; and the institution of stereotypic classifications, harassment, and oppression. Minority groups are those singled out due to culture, social standing, or physical characteristics.

- Four common classifications are: race, gender, sexual orientation and age.
- Five common racial groups are: Asian, Black, Hispanic/Latino, Native American and White.

- Issues of race involve: racism/racial bias and ethnocentrism, or believing that one's own race is superior.
- Issues of gender involve: "sexism," especially the subordination of women (being treated as if weak, intellectually inferior, and passive).
- Issues in sexual orientation involve: homophobia, or an irrational fear of gays and lesbians, and treatment-seeking concerns, such as stigmatization, internalized homophobia, fear of being "outed," and countertransference issues.
- Issues of ageism include: devaluation and stereotypes (asexuality, rigidity, cognitive decline, etc). Other minority groups include: the disabled and the indigent/poor.

Asians and Blacks

While generalizations can be helpful for a starting point, it is essential that clients not be stereotyped and that the social worker remains continually and entirely open to client differences. Culture-bound syndromes are symptoms that mimic a mental disorder (e.g., hallucinations and delusions) but that are rooted in cultural behavior. These must be ruled out and not diagnosed (see DSM-IV-TR Appendix I).

Common Asian traits include: the family is the basic unit, as opposed to the individual, the elderly, and oldest males in particular, are granted the greatest respect, there is a need to preserve "family honor", and there is usually considerable resistance to being open in personal matters with strangers.

Common Black traits include: there is a deep respect for the elderly, there are strong extended kinship ties, building rapport and making eye contact are important to securing trust, religion influences all facets of life, and empowerment and advocacy are often needed.

Native Americans and Hispanics

Common Native American traits include: the tribe makes all important decisions, child-rearing is often tribal, customs and tribal rituals must be honored, in many cases, tribes have their own laws and rules recognized by the government ("tribal sovereignty"), and substance abuse is often a significant issue.

Common Hispanic traits include: there is an emphasis on the importance of family, one turns to the family in times of distress (whether financial, social, or emotional) before seeking outside help, family leadership is patriarchal, with the father often making authoritative decisions, a sense of "machismo" is important for men, personal and social relations and networks are highly regarded, religion plays an important role, and speaking the native language and skilled nonverbal communication can be essential to successful engagement.

Understanding

Knowledge of human behavior is integral to social work practice. Thus, the first layer of understanding arises through the various theories that explain individual, institutional, community, and organizational behavior. Social workers must use these theories to better inform their understanding of diversity and behavior in ethnic groups. Second, ethnic self-awareness provides a greater understanding of the differences that must be surmounted and the barriers that these differences might impose. It also provides for a more empathetic relationship to be formed. The third layer is the impact of ethnic reality on daily life. Ethnic issues shape the psychological and social being in a multitude of ways. Individuals draw upon their culture-centered experiences and beliefs to aid them in times of crisis situations. How social workers view their clients often affects how the client will respond to any help offered. Thus, the social worker must understand the client's ethnic perspective to ensure a successful working relationship.

Assumptions

Certain key assumptions underlie an ethnic-sensitive social work practice. Fundamentally, the social worker must be aware of and sensitive to the history, values and perspectives of an ethnic group and how these elements affect each individual and the group as a whole. There are four main assumptions that inform a meaningful understanding of the influence of ethnicity.

- The history of the individual affects the perception, idea generation, and solution of problems.
- The effect of ethnicity on the here-and-now (the immediate present) is most important.
- Individual behaviors are affected by nonconscious (often ethnicity-sourced) phenomena.
- Influences of cohesion, identity, and strength make up the lived meaning of ethnicity, which may also cause strain, discordance, and strife. Thus, a meaningful understanding of a client's ethnicity, and most particularly its immediate impact on the client's life, can be essential to addressing any given problem or issue.

Important Skills

Cognitively, an ethnic-sensitive practice involves an understanding of the characteristics of the community, the agency context, and the ways of the target ethnic population. Further, social workers should know how a particular ethnic group deals with problems and should be familiar with referral networks and agencies specializing in serving the target population. Affectively, social workers should understand the fears that certain individuals might posses about receiving "outside" help. Behaviorally, when dealing with ethnic groups, social workers must use problem-solving skills that draw on fundamental understandings and facts about the group. Systemic sources of oppression should be noted and not allowed to affect ethnic groups that are already in danger of being oppressed.

Social workers must recognize that ethno-synchronous individuals with a greater number of resources are those who usually request help voluntarily from social workers. They are able to seek services without fear of being judged, critiqued, misunderstood, discriminated against, or burdened in some other similar way. Because of fears about being mistreated, oppressed ethnic groups often avoid seeking "outside" help for the problems they face. Indeed, it is often only when coerced to seek help by schools, courts, or other authoritative institutions that they present for assistance at all. Consequently, social workers need to be particularly cognizant of the concerns, fears, and apprehensions of individuals from diverse ethnic backgrounds, and endeavor to minimize these concerns by working responsively and empathetically with the issues that are identified.

Assessment in Social Work Practice

Client Assessment

Establishing rapport is the first step in client engagement (which often includes cursory exploration of the presenting problem), and this should be followed by explanations of the treatment process, ethical and legal obligations and limitations to confidentiality, etc. The next step is the completion of a written contract for services. It should specify the issues to be addressed, the goals to pursued, the roles and obligations of each party, and an anticipated course of treatment. Although reasonably explicit, the contract must also be flexible to allow for revision as needed.

The process of assessment is typically considered the first stage of treatment. Although it begins with the first session, it must continue throughout the course of treatment. During the assessment phase, data and information collection must take place to more fully illuminate the client's problem and any contributing factors. Common domains to be explored include: personal (emotional, intellectual, medical, etc.), family, social, community, employment, economic, legal, and religious/spiritual.

Assessment Methods

Assessments are ideally multidimensional and use a variety of methods. These may include the following methods: interviews (both verbal and written); indirect questioning (allusion, sentence completion, etc.); observation; client reports; and collateral contacts (agencies, family, medical providers, schools, etc.).

Common assessment approaches include:

- interviews: using both "open-ended" questioning (e.g., "What do you do in your free time?") and "closed-ended" questioning ("How old are you?")

- social assessment reports (social history): Past choices and conduct are the best predictors of future choices and conduct, thus history is important. The report contains basic facts, social data, the assessment and data interpretation.

- genograms: a "family tree" describing relationships in one or more generations

- ecomaps: a diagram locating a client in a social (including family) environment

- questionnaires: tools to prompt responses on key issues (depression, etc.)

- checklists: rapid response tools for summary issues (symptoms, etc.)

- mental status exams: cognitive evaluations

- intelligence tests

Suicide

The warning signs of suicide include:

- depression

- prior suicide attempts

- family suicide history

- abrupt increase in substance abuse

- reckless and impulsive behavior

- isolation

- poor coping

- support system loss

- recent or anticipated loss of someone special

- verbal expression of feeling out of control

- preoccupation with death

- behavior changes not otherwise explained

Where suicidality is suspected, the client should be questioned directly about any thoughts of self-harm. This should be followed by a full assessment and history (particularly family history of suicide, which is a significant predictor). Where the threat of suicide is not imminent and the client is amenable to intervention, a written "no-suicide contract" may be considered. In the contract, the client agrees to contact the suicide hotline, the social worker, or some other specified professional. Where a client already has a plan, or has multiple risk factors, hospitalization must be arranged. If any immediate attempt has already been made, a medical evaluation must occur immediately.

Abuse Evaluation

As mandated reporters, social workers must report all suspected cases of child abuse, as well as "dependent adult" and elder abuse. When assessing for signs of physical abuse, note particularly:
bruises, burns, cuts, or welts, and note if they are in various stages of healing; attempts by the victim to hide injuries; exaggerated efforts to please parents/caregivers; major behavioral problems or disturbances (violence, withdrawal, eloping, self-injury, etc.); and hypervigilance around adults, especially parents/caregivers.

Signs of psychological or emotional abuse include: depression, withdrawal, preoccupied with details, repetitive, agitated, and/or rhythmic movements, and evidence of unreasonable demands or conflict triangulation (e.g., drawing a child into marital conflicts).

Signs of neglect include: inappropriate dress, poor hygiene, failure-to-thrive symptoms (retarded development, underweight, hair loss, begging for food, etc.), poor supervision, significant fatigue, missed school and/or medical appointments, untreated health problems, and an inadequate sleeping situation.

Sexual Abuse

Common signs of sexual abuse include:

- genital injuries (abrasions, bruises, scars, tears, etc.)
- blood in the underwear (e.g., from vaginal and/or rectal injuries)
- complaints of genital discomfort and/or excessive grabbing of the genital area
- any diagnosis of a sexually transmitted disease
- frequent urinary tract and bladder infections
- complaints of stomach ache, when coupled with other signs
- abrasions or bruises to the thighs and legs
- enuresis (bed-wetting) and/or encopresis (fecal soiling)
- behavioral disturbances (acting out, self-destructive behavior, overly precocious and/or aggressive sexual behavior, promiscuity, etc.)
  - depression
  - eating disorders
  - fears and phobias
  - dissociation
  - any unexplained or sudden appearance of money, toys, or gifts

Follow-up

After abuse has been determined, a full report must be made to the appropriate agency, initially by telephone with a written report to follow. For social workers employed by such agencies, a follow-up plan of action must be determined. The level of risk must be evaluated, including the perpetrator's relationship to the victim, prior history of abusive behavior, and severity of harm inflicted, as well as the victim's age, health situation, cognitive capacity and psychological status, available support systems, and capacity for self-protection given that the abuse is now in the open. Options include: reports for criminal prosecution; home visits; removal from the home; and alternate caregiver/guardian appointments through the courts; etc. Safety is the primary concern, above all else.

DSM and ICD Manuals

The *Diagnostic and Statistical Manual of Mental Disorders* (DSM) is the accepted source for guidance in determining and documenting a proper psychiatric diagnosis. First published in 1952, the DSM has undergone many revisions, with the 2013 update DSM-5 (fifth revision) being the most recent. The DSM is similar in many ways to the current *International Classification of Disease* (ICD), now in its 10th edition with the "Clinical Modification" version (ICD-10-CM). The ICD also addresses psychiatric conditions. First published in 1948, the ICD has remained in continuous use worldwide. Today, however, the ICD text is most commonly used to classify diseases, syndromes, and conditions of all kinds for purposes of morbidity and mortality reporting as well as for epidemiological studies. Perhaps its most frequent use is for the classification of diseases and related treatments for purposes of insurance reimbursement.

DSM-IV-TR

The DSM-IV-TR uses a "multi-axial" approach to diagnosis. In a complete workup, all five axes are used to fully describe a client. Axis I addresses clinical disorders (e.g., depression), and major mental disorders such as bipolar disorder (manic-depression) and schizophrenia. Axis II addresses personality disorders (i.e., enduring dysfunctions in perception and responses) and intellectual disability. Axis III addresses physical disorders with bearing on a patient's status (e.g., diabetic neuropathy complicating depression). Axis IV addresses related psychosocial factors (e.g., divorce, retirement, illiteracy, victim of crime). Axis V, the Global Assessment of Functioning (GAF), is used to rate an individual's overall social, occupational, and psychological functioning. Based on a scale of 1 to 100, the GAF ranges from harming oneself or others (1–10) to having no symptoms/issues at all (91–100).

Diagnostic Codes

Entries on Axes I and II are assigned "codes" to identify each diagnosis, with added "severity" specifiers (e.g., mild, moderate, severe, in partial remission). These code entries must be justified through a supporting narrative. Tentative Axis I diagnoses (e.g., lacking essential features during an initial workup) may be noted by entering the code, followed by a "rule out" notation (e.g., "309.0: Adjustment Disorder with depressed mood; rule-out Dysthymic Disorder (300.4)), or by entering a "V code." V codes identify tentative conditions requiring clinical attention (or those not due to a mental disorder but still requiring clinical attention). These codes are entered on Axis I (except for V71.09, which may be entered on Axis I or II when it is a focus of clinical attention, or on Axis IV when it is not). Of additional note, Axis II disorders are not diagnosed at an initial workup, as a proper diagnosis can be made only after a sufficient passage of time. In the interim, entries typically appear as: "301.83: Borderline Personality Traits."

Childhood and Adolescence Disorders

Psychiatric disorders common to childhood and adolescence include:
- Attention deficit hyperactivity disorder (ADHD): persistent hyperactivity/impulsivity and/or inattention in two or more key situations (home, school, work) with symptoms present prior to 7 years of age (common medications: Ritalin, Cyclert)
- Autistic disorder: deficits in communication and social interaction, often including persistent repetitive behaviors such as head banging and/or rocking, with symptoms present before 3 years of age

- Conduct disorder: persistent violations of standards of proper behavior, including aggression toward people and animals, deceit, destruction of property, running away, theft, truancy, etc., in someone under the age of 18 (when over 18+, the behavior is diagnosed as antisocial personality disorder)
- Encopresis: persistent defecation in inappropriate places when over the age of 4
- Enuresis: persistent urination (whether voluntary or involuntary) when over the age of 5
- Separation disorder: exaggerated distress at separation from figures of attachment when under the age of 18
- Intellectual disability (also called developmental delay [DD]) refers to deficits in cognitive and adaptive function with symptoms evident before the age of 18. Causes include genetic factors, birth trauma, brain infections, exposure to toxins, and head trauma. An average intelligence quotient (IQ) score is 100, and low normal scores range from 85 to 99; borderline = 71–84; mild = (50–55) – 70; moderate = (35–40) – (50–55); severe = (20–25) – (35–40); profound = below (20–25).
- Oppositional defiant disorder (ODD) refers to an ongoing pattern of disobedient, defiant, and hostile behavior (e.g., argumentativeness, blaming, spitefulness, vindictiveness) toward those in authority sufficient to compromise function in social, academic, or occupational settings. However, the symptoms cannot be the result of another disorder, such as the more serious conduct disorder, depression, anxiety, psychosis, etc., with persistent evidence for at least six months.

Delirium vs. Dementia

The two most common causes of cognitive dysfunction are delirium and dementia, and both result in an inability to acquire, retain, and use knowledge normally. Delirium and dementia may coexist, but they are quite different. Diagnosis of delirium is based on clinical observation, as no diagnostic tests are available. The essential features are: acute onset (hours/days) and a fluctuating course, inattention or distraction, and an altered level of consciousness resulting in disorganized thinking. In contrast, dementia begins gradually, is slowly progressive, and is usually not reversible. The two disorders have different effects on cognitive function, as delirium is primarily a disturbance of attention while dementia disrupts primarily memory. While delirium and dementia may occur at any age, the conditions typically affect older people secondary to age-related changes in the brain. The diagnosis of delirium is missed more than 50% of the time.

Substance abuse vs. Substance Dependence

Substance abuse alone is considered a less severe condition than substance dependence. Substance abuse is diagnosed when major roles and obligations become impaired at home, school, and/or work; legal problems ensue (e.g., arrests for driving while intoxicated or disorderly conduct); and/or the abuse continues in spite of related interpersonal and social problems. Substance dependence refers to the increased use of a substance in order to achieve intoxication, withdrawal symptoms, and continued use in the face of efforts to stop. Medications often prescribed to reduce substance use include: Antabuse (disulfiram, which causes negative symptoms if alcohol is ingested) and ReVia and Trexan (both trade names for naltrexone, a reward/receptor blocker for alcohol and opiates).

Schizophrenia vs. Schizophreniform

In 1911 Eugene Bleuler coined the term "schizophrenia" and cited four key features (the "four A's"): autism (preoccupation with internal stimuli), affect disturbance (incongruent external manifestations of mood), association disturbance (illogical or fragmented thought processes), and ambivalence (simultaneous contradictory thinking). Common symptoms include delusions (false beliefs), hallucinations (false perceptions, e.g., hearing "voices"), verbal disorganization (jumbled or incoherent speech), and profoundly disorganized behavior or catatonia. The five types of schizophrenia are: catatonic (unresponsive, immobile, and often rigid and stiff; sometimes with peculiar movements such as grimacing or bizarre posturing), disorganized (confused or jumbled speech and behavior), paranoid (delusions of persecution or punishment), undifferentiated (symptoms of various types), and residual (symptoms still present but greatly reduced). A diagnosis of schizophreniform disorder is made if the symptoms exist longer than one month but less than six months (functional impairments are also usually much less).

Brief Psychotic Disorder vs. Schizoaffective Disorder

The condition of brief psychotic disorder is characterized by schizophrenic-like symptoms (delusions, hallucinations, disorganized and/or incoherent speech and significant behavioral disorganization, etc.) that last longer than one day but less than one month, after which a diagnosis of schizophreniform disorder would be considered. Schizoaffective disorder refers to a schizophrenic-like condition that occurs in concert with a mood disorder. Consequently, there are two primary subtypes: schizoaffective disorder, depressive type (characterized by schizophrenic symptoms coupled with major depressive symptoms only) and schizoaffective disorder, manic type (having symptoms that meet the diagnostic criteria for both schizophrenia and mania). Medications often prescribed for symptoms of psychosis include Clorazil, Haldol, Loxitane, Mellaril, Prolixin, Risperdal, Stelazine, Thorazine, and Zyprexa.

Mood Disorders

The diagnosis of major depression involves a depressed mood sufficient for the person to lose interest in nearly all activities and to incur weight loss or gain, insomnia or hypersomnia, a sense of helplessness and/or worthlessness, poor concentration, and/or thoughts about dying extending two weeks or more. A diagnosis of "with psychotic features" is added if symptoms of psychosis also appear. A diagnosis of mania is made when an individual experiences an exaggerated sense of mood (elation, expansiveness, or irritableness) that is characterized by insomnia, talkativeness, grandiosity, distractibility, and tangential "flights of ideas" for a period of at least one week. Psychotic features can occur in severe cases. A diagnosis of mixed mood disorder can be made where criteria for both severe depression and mania are met on most days for one week. A diagnosis of hypomania is given when the symptoms of mania are present but the episode is not severe enough to cause marked impairment in social or occupational functioning or to necessitate hospitalization, and there are no psychotic features.

Bipolar Disorders

Bipolar disorder refers to a cycling of mood, alternating between a normal state and mania and/or depression. The average frequency of episodes is 0.4 to 0.7 per year, lasting three to six months, though some may have a "rapid cycle." The cycles may vary in intensity and duration, from severe to mild, and last hours or even years if left untreated. There are four kinds of bipolar disorders:
bipolar I, at least one manic episode, with or without depressive symptoms; *bipolar II*, hypomanic episodes with at least one major depressive episode in the past; *cyclothymic disorder*, both depressive and hypomanic symptoms falling short of outright mania and major depression; and "*Bipolar Disorder, NOS*" (not otherwise specified), sometimes called "sub-threshold bipolar disorder," where cycling mood is evident but difficult to categorize. A diagnosis is posted by name, primary pole, variation, and severity (e.g., "Bipolar I Disorder, Manic Episode, Mixed, Moderate).

Depressive Disorders

Major depression involves the loss of interest in nearly all activities, along with weight loss or gain, insomnia or hypersomnia, a sense of helplessness and/or worthlessness, poor concentration, and/or thoughts about dying extending two weeks or more. There must be no history of manic, mixed, or hypomanic episodes. Dysthymic disorder ("chronic depression" or "minor depression") is a less severe depression but can be quite disabling. It involves depressive symptoms almost daily for at least two years (one year for children and adolescents), without meeting the criteria for a major depression. Low energy, sleep disturbances, changes in appetite, and low self-esteem are typically present as well. A medical evaluation is necessary to rule out physical causes. "Double depression" may occur in those with dysthymic disorder who later develop a major depressive episode. In such cases disorders are diagnosed. Once the major depressive episode resolves, and the dysthymic symptoms persist, only the dysthymic disorder is diagnosed.

Anxiety and Panic Disorders

Panic disorder symptoms include intense anxiety, chest tension, dizziness, nausea, rapid heart rate, shaking, trembling, feelings of depersonalization and loss of control, etc. Panic disorder without agoraphobia involves recurrent, unexpected panic attacks, often arising from the fear of having an attack. Panic disorder with agoraphobia refers to panic attacks in places where either escape or help in the event of an attack might not be possible, such as in crowds, on bridges, at social events, or even just being outside alone. Generalized anxiety disorder involves chronic and exaggerated worry and tension, often about health, money, family, work, etc. The diagnostic criteria include worry for more days than not for at least six months, symptoms of irritability, muscle tension, sleep disturbance, fatigue, and poor concentration. The worry must not arise from substance abuse, a medical condition, or other psychiatric disorders. Finally, it must cause significant distress or impairment in social, occupational, or other important areas of functioning. Common treatment medications include Celexa, Haldol, Klonopin, Librium, Paxil, Tofranil, Xanax, and Valium.

Phobias, Obsessive-Compulsive Disorder, and Posttraumatic Stress Disorder

There are many phobias caused by exposure to specific objects or situations that pose little real danger. Transient anxiety is common when giving a speech or taking a test. In contrast, a phobia is long-lasting and causes intense distress. It can disrupt normal function in occupational, school, or social settings. Social phobia is an exaggerated fear of social situations sufficient to cause functional impairment in daily life. Obsessive-compulsive disorder is diagnosed when obsessions (intrusive thoughts) and compulsions (behavioral urges) dominate an individual's life to the extent that academic, occupational, or social functioning is disrupted. Posttraumatic stress disorder refers to a constellation of symptoms following an event which threatens life or serious injury. Symptoms include recurrent intrusive recollections, dreams, anger, distraction, irritability, sleep disturbance, hypervigilance, and/or an exaggerated startle response. Common treatment medications include Celexa, Haldol, Klonopin, Librium, Paxil, Tofranil, Xanax, and Valium.

Somataform Disorders

Specific somatoform disorders include: somatization disorder, conversion disorder, pain disorder, hypochondriasis, and body dysmorphic disorder. Somatization disorder is relatively rare and involves several years of medical complaints before the age of 30 resulting in either unnecessary treatment or impaired functioning in social or occupational settings. Conversion disorder patients present with neurological symptoms such as numbness, blindness, deafness, paralysis, or fits, but also have positive physical signs of hysteria that have transformed intrapsychic distress into physical symptoms. Pain disorder involves symptoms of pain of a psychological origin. Hypochondriasis involves a belief that one has the symptoms of a medical illness, even after medical tests show that one does not. It often involves misinterpretation of minor health problems or normal body functions as symptoms. Body dysmorphic disorder involves a persistent preoccupation with an imagined defect in appearance or severity of a perceived physical flaw that impairs important life functions (e.g., work, school).

Factitious Disorder vs. Malingering

Factitious disorder (FD) involves: the deliberate generation or feigning of physical or psychological symptoms, a desire to assume the "sick role," and no outside motivation (e.g., no financial incentive and avoidance of responsibility and of enhancing health). There are three types of FD: FD with psychological symptoms, FD with physical symptoms, and mixed FD. The infamous "Munchausen syndrome" refers to a subset of patients exhibiting a chronic variant of FD with predominantly physical symptoms. FD by proxy (and the more severe "Munchausen by proxy")— involving the production or feigning of symptoms by one person in another (typically by a mother in a child) to assume the sick role by proxy (not for external gain)—has yet to be codified in the DSM-IV-TR, though Appendix B provides research criteria. "Malingering" is not a clinical diagnosis and instead refers to the production of physical symptoms explicitly for gain—to avoid work, to obtain insurance or disability benefits, to win a legal injury settlement case, etc.

Dissociative Disorders and Eating Disorders

Dissociative disorders include: dissociative identity disorder (previously "Multiple Personality Disorder"), where more than one distinct personality or identity assumes control of behavior (leaving the other(s) unable to recall involved events or the other identities); dissociative amnesia, where critical personal information (usually stressful or traumatic) is blocked out to escape associated distress; dissociative fugue, or a sudden and unexpected loss of awareness of self and surroundings, leaving the individual to depart on a journey for hours, days, or months; and depersonalization disorder, a feeling of detachment or distance from one's own experience, body, or self, as in a dream or being "spaced out." When this condition is severe, the external world appears unreal or distorted. Eating disorders include: anorexia nervosa, a distortion in body perception leading to a fear of weight gain, malnutrition, and amenorrhea in postmenarcheal females; and bulimia nervosa, binge eating followed by vomiting and/or laxative use to prevent weight gain.

Cluster A

Cluster A includes paranoid, schizoid, and schizotypal personality disorders. Paranoid personality disorder is characterized by a fundamental distrust of others coupled with a belief that others may well attempt to do them harm in one way or another. These people do poorly in close relationships because of their excessive suspiciousness and hostility, traits of which they are often poorly aware. Schizoid personality disorder is characterized by a consistent effort to avoid social activities and interaction with others. These people tend to be loners with a marked inability to form personal relationships. Schizotypal personality disorder is one of several eccentric personality disorders. People with schizotypal personality disorder are unable to form close relationships and tend to distort reality in ways somewhat like a mild form of schizophrenia. They exhibit odd behavior, in dress, speech, thoughts, beliefs (e.g., magical, fantasy, psychic, or superstitious preoccupations), and perceptions. They are extremely uncomfortable with intimacy and often come across as emotionally distant, aloof, or cold.

Cluster B

Cluster B includes antisocial, borderline, histrionic, and narcissistic personality disorders. Antisocial personality disorder is characterized by a gross disregard for the rights, feelings, safety, and property of others. Those with this disorder have a history of conduct disorder before age 15. Borderline personality disorder is characterized by a marked instability of relationships (alternating between overvalued and then profoundly devalued feelings for significant others) and an unstable self-image and affect, along with chronic feelings of emptiness and a high degree of impulsivity and self-entitlement. Histrionic personality disorder is characterized by significant attention-seeking behavior, along with highly volatile, exaggerated, and unstable emotions. Narcissistic personality disorder is characterized by a profound need for admiration, attention, and empathy from others, coupled with a grandiose sense of self that is far out of proportion to any related measure of personal accomplishment.

Cluster C

Cluster C includes obsessive-compulsive, avoidant, and dependent personality disorders. Obsessive-compulsive personality disorder is characterized by a preoccupation with rules, order, perfection, and control at the expense of flexibility, openness, and efficiency. This person is overly occupied with details, lists, organization, and/or schedules, has a tendency toward perfectionism that interferes with task completion, is overly focused on work and productivity to the exclusion of leisure activities and friendships, keeps worn-out/worthless objects lacking sentimental value, won't delegate unless others submit to exactly his/her way of doing things, and shows rigidity and stubbornness. Avoidant personality disorder is characterized by extreme shyness, feelings of inferiority, and a fear of rejection. Use caution in diagnosing children, adolescents, and others for whom shy and avoidant behavior may be appropriate (e.g., new immigrants). Dependent personality disorder is characterized by clingy, submissive, indecisive, and needy behaviors, thoughts, and emotions. This person needs others to assume responsibility and desperately needs supportive relationships.

Direct and Indirect Practice

Treatment Plan

The treatment plan is used to set goals and objectives and to monitor progress. Goals are considered broad-based aims that are more general in nature (e.g., becoming less anxious, developing improved self-esteem), while objectives are the fundamental steps needed to accomplish the identified goals. Because objectives are used to operationalize goals, they must be written with considerable clarity and detail (questions of who, what, where, when, why, and how should be carefully answered). Properly constructed objectives must be based upon the client's perceptions of needs, as opposed to a clinician's bias, whenever possible. Finally, the treatment plan should be revised and updated as often as necessary to ensure that it remains an effective guiding and monitoring tool.

Treatment Termination

Ideally, termination occurs voluntarily and after all treatment goals have been met, though involuntary and precipitous terminations sometimes occur (e.g., because of moves, limited insurance coverage). Where possible, the social worker and the client should collaborate on identifying a termination date, based upon goal attainment, support needs, etc. Termination typically involves goal review, along with discussion about plans for steps the client can take to maintain the progress achieved and to continue progress in identified areas needing further development. Clinicians should be aware that impending termination can elicit various client feelings, including sadness, anxiety, anger, rejection, and a sense of loss. Any such feelings should be thoroughly processed as a termination date approaches. Where overly intense client feelings arise, a follow-up meeting some weeks later may help. Regardless, the client should be reassured that he/she may return at any time.

Practice Frameworks

Social work "practice frameworks" serve as a frame of reference and basis from which to address client issues or problems. The criteria for selection of a practice framework include: the kind of problem that presents, the relevant psychological theoretical orientation, the form of treatment needed/available (e.g., individual, family, group), the outcomes/goals sought, and the available time and resources. The application of additional practice frameworks may be necessary over the course of the treatment process. Thus, the social worker should develop facility in multiple frameworks in order to facilitate client treatment and to meet the goals and needs of the agency or institution in which the social worker is employed.

The "generalist" framework is a broad, eclectic, flexible approach that is open to the application of multiple theories, models, and methods of intervention. At the opposite end of this continuum is the "specialist" approach, which would be limited to a single theoretical orientation and intervention approach. The "systems" framework engages the biological and social aspects of human behavior and focuses on the interface between the client's behavior and the social environment in relation to the presenting issue or problem. The "ecosystems" framework evaluates client behaviors from the perspective of environmental adaptation. The "ethnic-sensitive" framework places a client's culture, ethnicity, and religious perspectives central to the assessment and intervention process. The "feminist" framework is applied when issues of gender, roles, stereotyping, and discrimination are of primary concern. The "strengths" framework examines and capitalizes on a client's strengths to achieve the necessary outcomes.

Psychoanalytic Approach

The psychoanalytic (or psychodynamic) intervention approach draws upon psychoanalytic theory, ego psychology theory, psychosocial theory, and object relations theory. Key tenets of this intervention approach include:

- The social environment is the primary external influence.
- Behavior is seen as emerging from unconscious motives and drives.
- Dysfunction is rooted in stress-producing experiences and conflicts in the unconscious mind.
- Problem resolution is brought about by drawing repressed information into the conscious mind and using the energy from the stress of this process to overcome conflict and induce change.

Key barriers to this process are the defense mechanisms, as well as transference (the client's unconscious issues, feelings, desires, and defenses involving the social worker) and countertransference (the social worker's unconscious issues, feelings, desires, and defenses involving the client). The role of the social worker is focused on resolving conflict.

Psychoanalytic Assessment and Treatment Phases

From a psychoanalytic intervention approach, assessment is a continuous process throughout the treatment process. Key elements of assessment include: identifying and overcoming defense mechanisms that are barriers to progress, identifying and understanding the etiology of various conflicts impeding the change process (the how and why of the conflicts discovered), observing body language, verbal expressions, narration, and word selection in descriptions of life experiences to better identify unconscious motivations, drives, and other influences impacting the issue(s) of concern. The phases of treatment include: engagement (building trust and rapport), contracting (identifying goals, boundaries, and the course of treatment), ongoing treatment (issue resolution in a manner to optimize current functioning), and termination (reviewing and summarizing progress and planning future independent steps for progress maintenance and continued growth).

Psychoanalytic Treatment Techniques

The psychoanalytic approach uses numerous techniques in the treatment process, including: *free association* (encouraging a client to relate anything that comes to mind in order to examine unconscious thinking, distortions, hidden desires, etc.); *confrontation* (the bringing together of opposing ideas for purposes of exploration) to overcome "*resistance*" (client avoidance of difficult memories and experiences, resulting in delayed growth and progress); "*delving*" (exploring the client's past for clues to current circumstances, thinking, desires, fears, and motivations); *dream analysis* (analyzing and interpreting dreams in search of unconscious desires, fears, and motivations); *ventilation* (releasing difficult thoughts and emotions); *sustainment* (accepting, encouraging, reassuring to bolster client confidence); and *direct influence* (advising and encouraging specific behaviors and changes to achieve desired goals).

Behavioral Approach

The behavioral (or behavioral modification) intervention approach draws upon behavioral theory, classical (respondent) conditioning theory, operant conditioning theory, and social learning theory. Key tenets of this intervention approach include:

- The focus is on observable behavior as opposed to underlying emotions and mental disorders.
- Behavioral evaluation replaces exploration of the past or of the unconscious mind.
- Conscious choices to change are sufficient to overcome dysfunctional behaviors.

- Behavioral modification techniques can induce both conscious/voluntary change, and behavioral conditioning and reinforcement (i.e., combining dysfunctional behavior with a negative effect) can induce unconscious change.
- Change occurs only when behaviors are specifically identified, operationally defined, and coupled with consequences that can be controlled.
- Change is most rapid and enduring when the client voluntarily desires to change.

Behavioral Treatment Phases and Contracting

The phases of treatment involve: identifying dysfunctional behaviors, prioritizing behaviors in need of change, operationally defining the behaviors (identifying related antecedents and necessary consequences, putting change interventions into motion, monitoring for behavioral change for goal achievement, and identifying new antecedents and consequences for the next prioritized behavior targeted for change. Treatment contracting involves creating a formal agreement between the social worker and the client that specifically identifies the "target behavior," sets new behavioral antecedents and consequences (that are wholesome and functional), specifies the response to contract violations, specifies necessary positive reinforcers used to maintain desired behavioral change, specifies necessary negative reinforcers to be used if dysfunctional behaviors reemerge, and identifies the indices and methods of monitoring (tallies, charts, etc.) to evaluate the intervention process. The contract must be revised, renewed, and updated as necessary.

Behavioral Treatment Techniques

The role of the social worker is less significant in terms of the therapist-client relationship than that involved in a psychoanalytic approach. Even so, it should be supportive, understanding, and facilitative in order to sustain the difficult process of change. Treatment techniques in a behavioral approach largely involve the identification of the antecedents and consequences of dysfunctional behaviors in need of change, and the establishment of new antecedents and consequences to facilitate and maintain desirable changes. In this process, however, the social worker may also assign the client to maintain a "behavioral journal." In this journal, the client will make detailed notes about when dysfunctional behaviors occur, any evident triggers for the behavior, the feeling during and after the behavior, etc. In this way the frequency, intensity, and patterns associated with target behaviors can be identified and monitored. Reinforcement and conditioning techniques will then be implemented and refined to better reinforce desirable behaviors and extinguish dysfunctional behaviors.

Cognitive Approach

The cognitive approach derives its theoretical orientation from cognitive theory. Key features of this intervention approach include:

- A problem-focused, goal-oriented approach to the process of personal growth and change.
- A focus on the present as opposed to the past.
- A belief that all emotions and behaviors experienced and exhibited by an individual result from specific thoughts and processes of cognition.
- A belief that behavioral change results when an individual's false beliefs, distortions, and misconceptions are identified, challenged, and revised to produce more functional beliefs, emotions, thoughts, and behaviors.
- Incorporation of an educational component by which the client is taught how to identify and revise problematic thinking independently.

Cognitive Assessment and Treatment Phases

In the cognitive approach, the role of the social worker is educational, facilitative, and collaborative in pursuing and achieving the client's goals. The process of client assessment is focused on identifying and clarifying the client's specific false beliefs, distortions, and misconceptions as related to the area of concern. The phases of treatment following the assessment phase include in-depth issue clarification, goal setting, contracting between the social worker and client (formalizing agreements regarding the course of treatment, its scope, and overarching goals), education (regarding misconceptions, thought triggers, and resultant behaviors), cognitive reconstruction, progress monitoring, outcome evaluation, and treatment termination.

Cognitive Treatment Techniques

Treatment techniques utilized in the cognitive approach include: *clarification*: feedback to aid the client to see misperceptions, distortions, and false beliefs more clearly; explanation: educating the client to better recognize, understand, and correct cognitive errors, along with the identification of triggers and related thought processes and behaviors that must be dealt with for problem resolution to occur; *interpretation*: providing extrapolative explanations and theoretical linkages to enhance insight and understanding; writing assignments: a process by which the client deconstructs misperceptions, distortions, and false beliefs, usually by writing down a description of events and/or thoughts and then examining the narrative for accuracy and rationality; *paradoxical direction*: directing the client to pursue the specific behavior targeted for change to increase awareness and enhance the client's sense of control over it; and *reflection*: stimulating a client to examine relevant feelings and thoughts to enhance understanding and insight.

Gestalt Approach

The Gestalt approach derives its theoretical orientation from Gestalt theory. Key features of this intervention approach include:
- The premise that every individual has the capacity for growth and change.

- Awareness that the feelings related to any given change can facilitate the change process.
- Treatment that remains client focused (not problem focused).
- Awareness of the "whole self" (the inner and outer self, one's past experiences, and the lived environment) as being essential to change.
- Taking responsibility for the behaviors we choose to the extent that we become aware of and understand those behaviors.
- Awareness that current personal behaviors will lead naturally to the selection of enhanced behaviors as the individual begins to understand and take responsibility for the consequences of those behaviors.

Gestalt Assessment and Treatment Phases

The role of the social worker in Gestalt therapy is that of a facilitator in aiding the individual to become more holistically aware of the self, as it is assumed that the individual already possesses all the necessary tools for change and growth once awareness is expanded and the need for personal responsibility is clear. This requires a positive, supportive, and warm working relationship. Assessment focuses on the level of a client's awareness and insights into personal understanding. The Gestalt approach departs from other therapy forms in that assessment need not focus on a client's cognitive, emotional, physical, psychological, or social condition, or on a DSM-IV-TR diagnosis. These are superfluous to the change process, which requires only individual awareness and insight into behavioral responsibility. Treatment phases, however, are similar to those seen in other approaches, including the identification of presenting problems/issues, setting goals, and contracting together regarding the goals, course, and scope of treatment.

Gestalt Treatment Techniques and Conceptual Barriers

Treatment techniques and concepts utilized in the Gestalt approach include: *dialogue* (the "empty chair" technique), where the client is directed to communicate with someone with whom conflict exists but who is not actually present; *enactment of dreams*: the acting out of key features of a dream; *rehearsal*: the process of practicing a certain feeling, thought, or behavior in preparation for change; *exposing the obvious*: bringing certain thoughts, actions, or statements originating with the client to his/her awareness; and *exaggeration*: a dramatization of some physical or verbal action in order to enhance awareness.

Key conceptual barriers to change include: *confluence*: an unrealistic emphasis on similarities to the overreduction or exclusion of differences; *introjection*: the inappropriate acceptance and internalization of messages from others; *projection*: attributing the unacceptable or undesirable aspects of one's own personality to another individual; and *retroflection*: doing to oneself what one wishes to do to another.

Task-Centered Approach

The task-centered approach derives its theoretical orientation from behavioral theory, cognitive theory, and social learning theory. Key features of this intervention approach include:

- The focus is on solely behavioral issues that the client wishes to change, rather than on those that the social worker views as in need of change.
- Behaviors are chosen and perpetuated by the individual, rather than behavior arising from influences of the environment or through learning.
- All behaviors are made consciously and are entirely controlled by the individual, who is capable of changing them.

- The desire to change is central to success (clients treated involuntarily would not fully benefit).
- Change is facilitated when the social worker suggests helpful environmental changes, supports client self-esteem, and clarifies the problem and the objectives needed for its resolution.
- Treatment is short term: 6–12 sessions over a period of several months.

Task-Centered Assessment and Treatment Phases

The role of the social worker is primarily facilitative and supportive in assisting the client as requested without interjecting hidden goals or agendas. Assessment focuses on evaluating client-selected behaviors for change, identifying change barriers and associated behaviors, and refining goals and relevant objectives. Phases of treatment involve goal identification, objective clarification (e.g., steps to achieve the goals), the development of a formal contract (with detailed content covering behavioral goals, steps for change, treatment duration, and cost, revised as needed), treatment, and termination. Treatment involves identification of skills and actions for task accomplishment practice by the client (both during and between sessions), progress review, and treatment plan revision. Termination occurs in accordance with the contract and involves progress review and finalizing plans to maintain and further the change process. Direct treatment techniques are typically drawn from behavioral or cognitive-behavioral therapy.

Crisis Intervention

Crisis intervention derives its theoretical orientation from ego psychology, psychoanalytic theory, and social learning theory. Key tenets include:
- Interventions are limited to a time of crisis, defined as any highly stressful, disturbing, or disastrous event that leaves an individual unable to cope using existing coping resources.

- A crisis tends to elicit unpredictable behaviors and responses, leaving the individual uniquely malleable to intervention and change.
- A series of predictable stages ensues (the "crisis sequence"): the crisis event, feelings of anxiety and vulnerability when coping skills are overwhelmed, the "last straw" factor or event that causes a search for help, emotional turmoil and disequilibrium, and engagement of new coping skills, leading to crisis resolution.
- Individuals in crisis may not be "dysfunctional" (e.g., need no DSM-IV-TR diagnosis).
- The goal is to enhance coping capacity (not affect a "cure"); other life issues are dealt with only if related to the current crisis.
- Crisis intervention is short term and terminates when the immediate crisis is resolved.

Crisis Intervention Assessment and Treatment Phases

The social worker should have specific expertise in the crisis area (grief, rape, etc.), and should present as authoritative and direct in order to enhance client stability and reduce feelings of vulnerability. Care should be taken to prevent overattachment of the client to the social worker. The nature of a crisis limits the time available for assessment, which must thus be focused on the immediate issues. However, it should include exploration of the events surrounding the crisis, the client's current responses and past response patterns in similar situations, and available support systems and resources. Treatment involves examination of the precipitating events, the thoughts and emotions evoked, the skills needed to cope, and the development of sufficient supports and resources to facilitate crisis resolution. Treatment techniques may vary but tend to involve problem-solving strategies.

Grief Counseling

Grief counseling is short term and may utilize a variety of theoretical orientations derived from both communication theories and sociological concepts. Key tenets of this intervention approach include:

- Grief is a normal response at times of significant loss.
- Individuals typically pass through five stages of grief to reconcile a loss (Kubler-Ross, 1969):denial, a defense mechanism that protects an individual from the full initial impact of the loss; anger, at the irretrievability of the loss; bargaining, considering all "what if" and "if only" elements that could have prevented or could restore (appeals to God, etc.) the loss; despair/depression, as the full meaning of the loss emerges; and acceptance, surrendering to loss and coming to believe in eventual recovery.
- Individuals must eventually pass through all grief stages (some more briefly than others) for recovery to occur, often repetitively engaging various stages at various times and in varying order according to their needs and coping capacity at the time.

Family Therapy Approach

The family therapy approach derives its theoretical orientation from a variety of communication theories and sociological concepts. Key concepts of this intervention approach include:

- The family system is intended to be a source of affection, comfort, nurturance, and security.
- Family dysfunction can impact an individual both personally and socially.
- The family comprises three subsystems: the spousal subsystem, the parent–child subsystem, and the sibling subsystem.
- Each subsystem can affect both of the others, as well as the entire family system, when dysfunction or conflict is present.

- To be effective, treatment should be directed at a presenting problem, rather than attempting to engage all issues that may arise.
- Effective treatment will clarify roles and relationships and improve the quality of intrafamilial communication.

Family Therapy Assement and Treatment Phases

The role of the social worker is to educate, facilitate, and serve as a role model. Although actively involved in the therapeutic process, the social worker should remain neutral and direct the family members' attention toward each other in order to observe their patterns of interaction with each other. Assessment is ongoing and primarily involves observations regarding functional and dysfunctional aspects of the family system and subsystems. The phases of treatment include problem identification, goal setting, contracting, and termination. Types of therapies utilized include: family therapy: treating the family as a whole, to improve patterns of interaction and overall functioning; collaborative therapy: individual family member treatment by two or more clinicians, coordinating their efforts; complementary therapy: a family or group therapy adjunct to individual therapy (e.g., treating a family member for anger issues may involve referring the client to an anger management or family therapy group).

Family Therapy Treatment Techniques

Treatment approaches used in family therapy include: *the communications approach*, derived from the concept that poor communication is inherent in family dysfunction and requiring the social worker to prompt family members to listen more carefully and express themselves more plainly, openly, and honestly; *the strategic family therapy approach*, which requires the social worker to select and apply strategies to overcome and enhance previously poor family patterns of behavior and dysfunctional family rules; *the structural approach*, which calls for structural clarification of the roles, expectations, and responsibilities of all family members; *the social learning approach*, which focuses on developing family skills in communication and conflict resolution, while also enhancing patterns of family behavior through behavioral therapy strategies; *the narrative approach*, which derives from the concept that dysfunctional thinking and behaviors are rooted in deep-seated ideas, thoughts, and conceptions derived from personal stories (e.g., "narratives") and that change is achieved by the fabrication of new stories or alternate endings to previously handicapping narratives.

Group Therapy Approach

The group therapy approach derives its theoretical orientation from a variety of sources, including behavioral theory, cognitive theory, Gestalt theory, and psychoanalytic theory. Individuals may attend groups voluntarily (e.g., as recommended by a social worker) or involuntarily (by court order, etc.). Voluntary participation is typically the most effective. Key concepts of group therapy include:

- Not all issues and individuals are well suited to group processes. Some issues are too personal or complex, and some individuals are too uncomfortable or disruptive.
- Specific benefits typically accrue, such as: sharing with those who are coping with similar issues and experiences, which can be particularly supportive, as participants readily identify with each other; mutual comfort, derived from a sense of shared challenges; and lower levels of stress and intimidation, because of group support influences.
- Group therapy is typically a "complementary therapy" to individual therapy, rather than the sole treatment experience in itself.

Groups

Seven major types of groups are: *educational groups*, organized to teach and share skills and information on a specific topic (e.g., single parenting); *growth groups*, organized to enhance individual experience, understanding, and other measures of personal growth and development. Participants need not have any pathology, where overall growth or personal improvement is the goal; *remedial groups* (or "psychotherapy groups"), which provide support, treatment, and motivation for change in a specific area (e.g., anger management, obsessive-compulsive behavior); *self-help groups*, which empower individuals to make essential change through the encouragement of others seeking similar progress (e.g., Alcoholics Anonymous); *socialization groups*, which facilitate the enhancement of interpersonal skills, often using games and recreational activities; *support groups* (or "mutual sharing groups"), which facilitate participant sharing, encouragement, information exchange, etc., among those with common concerns (e.g., widows, single parents); and *task groups*, created to facilitate the achievement of a specific goal (e.g., developmentally delayed adults learning to live independently).

Group Structures

Groups may have varying structures. These include: *closed groups*: highly controlled groups with criteria for membership, size, location, number of sessions, etc. (e.g., a 10-week grief group), where new members are not allowed, providing a more intimate, cohesive group structure; *open groups*: loosely structured, with members who have made no commitment and may join or leave at any time (e.g., weight-loss groups); *short-term groups*: one to a few meetings for a particular event or purpose (pregnancy, parenting, etc.); *natural groups*: a collection of individuals formed informally (recently divorced friends, etc.) joined later by a social work facilitator; and *formed groups*: created purposely and specifically for a common issue or goal (e.g., a court-ordered drunk driving group).

Group Settings

The role of the social worker in a group has many facets, including: facilitator for gatekeeping (screening new members), reducing attrition, keeping group dynamics "safe" (preventing subgrouping, scapegoating, etc.), providing supplemental education, etc.; fostering a nurturing and successful learning environment; providing and modeling unconditional positive regard for all members; providing individual support: knowing all members' names, accommodating cultural issues, showing respect, etc.; building group cohesion, modeling inclusiveness via direct eye contact (where culturally appropriate), and showing meaningful attentiveness to all participating; using self-disclosure only where appropriate, only later (after trust exists), and only for the benefit of the group (rather than to meet self-needs) by determining the timing and purpose of any disclosures in advance and with a clear purpose; and using body language that is inclusive and open (facing the members, sitting in the circle, arms not crossed over the chest, etc).

Proper Group Formation

The following criteria should guide group formation: A balance between homogeneity and heterogeneity is necessary for both variety and cohesion—sharing common goals yet with different life experiences and backgrounds. Size should be considered relative to the topic and purpose of the group, ideally between 8 and 12 members (youth groups should be smaller—pre-adolescent groups: 3–4 members; teen groups: 6–10 members; adults 8–12 members), allowing for intimacy, trust, and variety. Composition criteria include ensuring that there is more than one individual of any particular race, gender, sexual orientation, etc. Even numbers limit the likelihood of "odd-one-out" pairs developing. The group's focus should be specific enough to ensure consistency of purpose, with similar intellectual levels, language, and experiences among the membership to facilitate bonding and group progress. Available resources and member capacity (age, health, mobility, etc.) should be considered in determining group location, costs, session numbers, and meeting length.

Group Treatment Phases

The first phase of treatment is the "engagement phase," including: gaining members commitment to attend and participate and contracting a clear and complete statement of each member's commitment to participate and the social worker and agency's commitment to remain involved, along with a clearly focused purpose (generally, the more specialized and focused, the greater the group's success). Assessment is ongoing, following group processes, dynamics, needs, and goals.

The middle phase includes: refining the group's purpose, ensuring successful group mechanics and comfort, and enhancing purposeful, valued, and productive group interactions.

The ending phase includes: early planning for termination, leaving ample time for all group members to come to grips with closure and separation and finalizing group goals and identifying goals that should continue beyond the group's existence.

Group Development and Treatment Concepts

Groups tend to move through five developmental stages: *preaffiliation*: becoming acquainted and deciding whether or not to participate; the group turns to the facilitator for considerable direction; *power and control*: group member roles form, and natural leaders emerge; challenges for power may occur; *intimacy*: bonding begins and appreciation and respect grow for the unique problems each member faces; *differentiation*: greater diversity of opinion emerges, and variations in thoughts and behaviors become evident; and *separation*: termination occurs, goals should be reviewed, and moving forward should be discussed, allowing for feelings of loss.

Key treatment concepts: The group facilitator should elicit participation from everyone in the group and keep some members from dominating. Group cohesion benefits group warmth, stability, cooperation, norming (adherence to group rules and standards), communication, and attendance. Scapegoating is unfair displacement of criticism and conflict on a vulnerable group member and is not to occur. Sociograms, or charts to depict relationships between group members, are used to analyze group processes and to plan improvements.

Horizontal and Vertical Approach

Social workers may be called upon to work for change and progress in large systems, such as in school districts, multi-site agencies, and communities and with governmental entities. In such situations, there are two key approaches: the "*horizontal approach*" and the "vertical approach" to engagement and intervention. The horizontal approach is used in working with centralized agencies and in communities. It involves bringing key participants ("stakeholders") into the process of problem identification, consensus building, goal setting, and implementation and monitoring of an improvement process. The *vertical approach* is used when there is a need to reach outside or beyond the community or centralized entity environment. This approach involves learning about hierarchical levels of leadership in government, charitable organizations, grant-funding institutions, etc., and then collaborating with key leaders in problem identification, consensus building, goal setting, and program implementation and monitoring to achieve the necessary goals. An understanding of systems theory and eco-systems (or life model) theory can aid in this process.

Systems Theory

Systems theory derives its theoretical orientation from "general systems theory," including elements of organizational theory, family theory, group behavior theory, and a variety of sociological constructs. Key principles include:

- Systems theory endeavors to provide a methodological view of the world by synthesizing key principles from its theoretical roots.

- A fundamental premise is that key sociological aspects of individuals, families, and groups cannot be separated from the "whole" (i.e., aspects that are "systemic" in nature).

- All systems are interrelated, and change in one will produce change in the others.

- Systems are either "open" or "closed": open systems accept outside input and accommodate, while closed systems resist outside input due to rigid and impenetrable barriers and boundaries.

- "Boundaries" are lines of demarcation identifying the outer margins of the system being examined.

- "Entropy" refers to the process of system dissolution or disorganization.

- "Homeostatic balance" refers to the propensity of systems to reestablish and maintain stability.

Eco-Systems Theory

- Eco-systems (or "life model") theory derives its theoretical orientation from ecology, systems theory, psychodynamic theory, behavioral theory, and cognitive theory. Key principles include:

- There is an interactive relationship between all living organisms and their environment (both social and physical).

- The process of adaptation is universal and is a reciprocal process by individuals and environments mutually accommodating each other to obtain a "goodness of fit."
- Changes in either individuals or their environments (or both) can be disruptive and produce dysfunction.
- Eco-systems theory works to optimize goodness of fit by modifying perceptions, thoughts, responsiveness, and exchanges between clients and their environments.
- On a larger (community) level, treatment interventions by the eco-systems approach are drawn from direct practice and include educating, identifying and expanding resources, developing needed policies and programs, and engaging governmental systems to support requisite change.

Communication

Reporting Abuse

Social work is one of several professions that are under legal "mandate" to report cases of abuse. It is not necessary to have witnessed the abuse, nor must one have incontrovertible evidence. Rather, there need only be sufficient cause to "suspect" in order for a report to be required. If the report is made "in good faith," the reporting party is immune from liability—both from reporting (should the allegations prove unfounded) and from the liability that would otherwise accrue from any failure to report actual abuse. Abuse may be physical, emotional, sexual in nature, or constitute neglect. All states mandate the reporting of child abuse, and most mandate the reporting of "dependent adult" abuse (adults who are developmentally delayed and thus mentally infirm or elderly persons unable to protect themselves due to either physical or mental frailty). Where dependent abuse reporting is not mandated, complex situations may occur. Know your state's laws and seek advice when necessary.

Managing Suicidality

Every state has laws addressing the requirements for clinicians in situations where a client exhibits a clear, foreseeable, and imminent threat of harm to him/herself. If an individual is discovered to be actively suicidal, a clinician can endeavor to dissuade the individual from acting upon his or her thoughts. "Contracting" may then follow (where the clinician may elicit promises and agreements from an individual about steps to take before acting upon any threat. Determinations of lethality are made based upon history, specificity of threats, whether the means are available, and the degree of planning already invested in carrying out the plan. Where the individual cannot be dissuaded from the suicidal threats and/or where the indices of lethality are high, law enforcement and certain designated mental

- 64 -

health professionals are empowered to involuntarily detain such individuals pending a more lengthy evaluation and subsequent legal review if the threat of suicide actively continues.

Managing Homicidality

A client may be deemed a threat to others if he or she makes a serious threat of physical violence and the threat is made against a specifically named individual(s). If the threat is also made in the context of a clinician–patient relationship, then a "duty to protect" is also generated. In such a situation, a clinician is duty bound not only to notify appropriate authorities and agencies charged to protect the citizenry, but to also make a good-faith effort to warn the intended victim(s) or, failing that, someone who is reasonably believed able to warn the intended victim(s). The duty to warn stems from the 1976 legal case *Tarasoff v. Regents of the University of California,* where a therapist heard a credible threat and called only law enforcement authorities, failing to notify the intended victim. The murder occurred, and the case was appealed to the California Supreme Court, from which the rubric of duty to protect an intended victim has been established.

Effective Communication

Communication involves the conveying of information, whether verbally or nonverbally between individuals. Communication can be divided into two key aspects: sending information and
receiving information. Each aspect requires unique skills, and effective communication requires proficiency in both. Essential principles include:

- All aspects of communication must be accounted for in any exchange.
- Communication may be written, verbally spoken, or nonverbally delivered via body language, gestures, and expressions.

- Not all communication is intentional, as unintentional information may also be conveyed.
- All forms of communication have limits, further imposed by issues of perception, unique experiences, and interpretation.
- Quality communication accounts for issues of age, gender, ethnicity/culture, intellect, education, primary language, emotional state, and belief systems.
- Optimum communication is "active" (or "reflective"), using strategies such as: furthering responses (nodding, etc.); paraphrasing; rephrasing; clarification; encouragement ("tell me more"); partialization (reducing long ideas into manageable parts); summarization; feelings reflection; exploring silence; and, nonverbal support (eye contact, warm tone, neutral but warm expressions, etc.).

Quality Communication Rules

When engaging a client, adhere to the following rules: Don't speak for the client (finishing sentences, etc.), instead allow the client to fully express him/herself. Listen carefully and endeavor diligently to understand. Don't talk when the client is speaking. Don't embellish; digest what the client has actually said, not what you presume was said. Don't interrupt, even if the process is slow or interspersed with long pauses. Don't judge, criticize, or intimidate when communicating. Facilitate communication with open-ended questions and a responsive and receptive posture. Avoid asking "Why" questions which can be perceived as judgmental. Communicate using orderly, well-planned ideas, as opposed to rushed statements. Moderate the pace of your speech, and adjust your expressions to fit the client's education, intellect, and other unique features. Ask clarifying questions to enhance understanding. Attend to nonverbal communication (expression, body language, gestures, etc.). Limit closed-ended and leading questions. Avoid "stacked" (multi-part) questions that can confuse.

There are many reasons to limit a client's opportunities to speak. Time may be short, the workload may be impacted, the client may seem distracted or uninterested in sharing, etc. However, only by allowing the client to divulge his or her true feelings can you actually know and understand what the client believes, thinks, feels, and desires. Barriers to client sharing include: frequent interruptions: instead, you might jot a short note to prompt your question later; supplying client words: a client may seem to have great difficulty finding words to express his/her feelings and you may be tempted to assist. However, this may entirely circumvent true expression, as the client may simply say, "Yes, that's it," rather than working harder to find his/her true feelings; filling silence: long "pregnant pauses" can be awkward. You may wish to fill the silence, but in so doing you may prevent the client from finding thoughts to share. Avoid these pitfalls to quality communication.

Informed Consent

Informed consent requires that no agreement to receive any treatment will be deemed valid unless sufficient information has been provided to achieve meaningful consent. The information provided should include the potential risks (both if the treatment is refused and if the treatment is provided), the hoped-for benefits, and the associated costs, and the available options should be reviewed. While every remote potential eventuality and outcome cannot always be addressed, the information presented should include that which a "reasonable person" would expect in the presenting circumstances. Simply delivering information, however, is not sufficient to secure genuine informed consent. The client must also be helped to understand the information in language and with examples appropriate to his or her intellectual capacity, primary language and communication skills, and educational background. Where an individual lacks the capacity for consent (e.g., a minor, a developmentally delayed adult, a cognitively impaired frail elder, someone suffering from mental illness), informed consent from a legal guardian should be obtained.

Active Listening Techniques

Active listening techniques include the use of paraphrasing in response, clarification of what was said to you, encouragement ("tell me more"), etc. Key overarching guidelines include: Don't become preoccupied with specific "active listening strategies"; rather, concentrate on reducing client resistance to sharing, building trust, aiding the client in expanding his/her thoughts, and ensuring mutual understanding. The greatest success occurs when a variety of active listening techniques are used during any given client meeting. Focus on listening and finding ways to help the client to keep talking. Active listening skills will aid the client in expanding and clarifying his/her thoughts.

Remember that asking questions can often mean interrupting. Avoid questioning the client when he or she is midstream in thought and is sharing, unless the questions will further expand the sharing process.

Nonverbal Communication

To facilitate the sharing process, it is important for a social worker to present as warm, receptive, caring, and accepting of the client. However, the social worker should also endeavor not to bias, lead, or repress client expressions by an inappropriate use of nonverbal cues. Frowning, smiling, vigorous nodding, etc., may all lead clients to respond to the social workers' reactions rather than to disclose their genuine feelings and thoughts. To this end, a social worker will endeavor to make good eye contact, use a soft tone of voice, present as interested and engaged, etc., but without marked expressions that can influence the dialogue process. Sitting and facing the client (ideally without a desk or other obstruction in between), being professionally dressed and groomed, sitting close enough to be engaging but without invading another's "space," and using an open posture (arms comfortable in your lap or by your sides, rather than crossed over your chest) can all facilitate the communication process.

Leading Questions

Leading questions are inquiries that predispose a particular response. For example, saying, "You do know that it is okay to ask questions, don't you?" is a powerful leading question. While it may seem an innocuous way to ensure that someone feels free to ask questions, it may not succeed in actually eliciting questions. Instead, ask the client directly, "Do you have any questions?" This inquiry not only reveals that questions are acceptable, but is much more likely to encourage the client to openly share any confusion he or she is having. Even less forceful leading questions can induce a bias. For example, when a couple comes in for counseling, asking, "Do you want to sit over here?" could prevent you from seeing how they elect to arrange themselves in relation to you and each other (a very revealing element in the relationship). Instead, you might simply say, "Feel free to sit anywhere you'd like." Avoiding leading questions is an important skill in the communication process.

Professional Relationships

Social Work Roles

Social workers may serve in many roles, including:

- Administrator: evaluating and developing policies and managing programs
- Advocate: defending, representing, and supporting vulnerable clients
- Broker: providing resource and service linkages to individuals in need
- Case manager: connecting, coordinating, and monitoring client services
- Counselor: exploring, treating, and resolving client, family, and/or group issues and problems
- Educator and teacher: researching and providing educational information, organizing and leading classes, teaching knowledge, skills, and/or behaviors that facilitate successful coping, growth, and relationships
- Lobbyist or politician: working to identify, understand, and resolve problems in local communities or in society as a whole by garnering support from key interest groups to marshal and wield influence for positive and necessary change.

Boundaries

In social worker–client relationships, the following principles apply: The Code of Ethics should guide proper professional boundaries. It is never proper to pursue or allow nonprofessional, social, recreational, or personal relationships with clients. Cite the Code of Ethics, if necessary, to avoid communicating rejection. Any gift, beyond a small token, should be politely and thoughtfully declined, citing the professional Code of Ethics, if necessary. Intimate relationships between social workers and clients (whether sexual or just overly close) are never appropriate. If a social worker develops unexpected feelings, supervisory consultation should be sought to evaluate the situation and consider assigning an alternate social worker.

Those in private practice may need to refer the client to another clinician. Confidentiality is a bedrock principle, and care should be taken to preserve it—with exceptions limited to reportable abuse (including credible threats to the client or others), court subpoena, case transfer, or limited cross coverage.

Agency Staff and Board Members Relationship

The board of directors oversees the development of policies by agency administrators, and the staff of the agency carries out the policies as approved. The board must hold the staff accountable for the implementation of the policies, because policy operationalization may utilize a variety of potential pathways. Administration evaluates the staff, and the performance of the staff ultimately reflects on the agency, which in turn reflects on the board. Representative staff members have the right to communicate with the board about any problems they face in implementing the policies. Open lines of communication between the board and the staff ensure success in the agency. The board, administration, and staff should have a triangular relationship based on clear job descriptions that state the responsibilities of each.

Case Managers and Direct Service Agency Relationship

The goal of case management is to ensure that clients with multiple issues receive the comprehensive services and aid they need in a timely and effective manner. The case manager does not provide direct services; instead, the case manager connects the client to direct service providers. The case manager is responsible for all the services provided by the direct service agency engaged. Thus, the case manager and the agency staff need a close working relationship, to ensure that all client needs are being met. While all areas of health and human services use case managers, they are especially utilized for the mentally ill, the elderly, and the disabled, as well as in matters of child welfare. Having one case manager responsible for all the needs of a client provides the client with the one-on-one attention needed and prevents the client from falling between the cracks when many direct service people are involved.

Interorganizational Relationships

It has been noted that the health care and social welfare fields often remain poorly integrated in the larger community networks and systems. Social work agencies need to better coordinate and build partnerships to more fully meet the needs of their individual clients and the community at large. One barrier to interorganizational relationships is the allocation of resources, as funds for both health care and social services are limited. A related concern is the interpenetration of organizational boundaries, often established to preserve resources, the client base, etc. Consequently there is often conflict within and between agencies on how best to proceed to the next level of service and who will be primarily responsible, etc. One way to overcome past divisiveness is to have shared memberships in key planning processes, by which to map the flow of care from one level to the next. Further, always central to this process is the need to enhance how different agencies communicate with one another to provide cohesiveness and continuity.

Professional Values and Ethics

Cultural Competence

- Ethics and values: Know the relevant standards in the profession and incorporate them into practice.
- Self-Awareness: Obtain a greater insight into one's own beliefs and culture, by which to better appreciate diversity in others.
- Cross-cultural knowledge: Develop the knowledge and insight into other cultures in order to better meet their needs.
- Cross-cultural skills: Develop the skills needed to work with diverse clients.
- Service delivery: Obtain enhanced knowledge of culturally diverse resources for better referrals.
- Empowerment and advocacy: Become aware of the impact of policies and programs on diverse clients, and advocate for those clients, as necessary.
- Diverse workforce: Recruit, hire, and retain ethnically diverse employees.
- Professional education: Attend educational events to advance cultural competence.
- Language diversity: Provide information and services in the client's language.
- Cross-cultural leadership: Share insights regarding diverse clients with other professionals to advance understanding.

Mission and Core Values

The National Association of Social Workers (NASW) describes the mission of social work as being the enhancement of human well-being and assisting individuals to secure their basic human needs in society. The professional focus of social work is on the individual in the context of society and the social and environmental forces involved in the problems of everyday life. The Code of Ethics identifies certain professional core values, which include: competence, human relationships, individual dignity, integrity, service, and social justice. A "client" is the focus of intervention, treatment, advocacy, support, etc., and could be an individual, family, group, community, or organization. The mission of social workers is to promote growth, well-being, and social justice on behalf of their clients.

Responsibilities to Clients

A social worker's ethical responsibilities to clients include: keeping the client's interests paramount and promoting client well-being; honoring and promoting client self-determination (limited only if client choices present a serious, foreseeable, and imminent risk of danger, to either the client or others); securing "informed consent," i.e., ensuring that treatment choices are made only after all reasonably possible risks, benefits, burdens, costs, and options have been explained to and understood by the client; providing only those services in which the social worker is experienced, competent, an authorized by virtue of education, licensure, and/or certification; providing culturally sensitive services; avoiding conflicts of interest that may compromise judgment or bias services, even if termination is subsequently required; not providing independent services to clients related to each other (e.g., couples, family members, etc.); avoiding multiple relationships with a client (e.g., counselor and fiduciary, conservator, etc.); the preservation of client privacy (except where reportable abuse or threat of abuse, subpoena, referral, and/or cross-coverage otherwise requires); disclosing confidential information only when and to the extent required by law; ensuring that clients have appropriate and timely access to their records; scrupulously avoiding all inappropriate physical contact with clients (e.g., close hugging, kissing, overly familiar touching, sexual contact); providing clients with a relationship that is free from all sexual harassment; setting fees with consideration for fairness and in the context of the client's ability to pay; ensuring service continuity; and ensuring that services are terminated when the client no longer needs the services being provided.

Responsibilities to Colleagues

Social worker ethical responsibilities to colleagues, as defined by the Code of Ethics of the National Association of Social Workers (NASW) include: ensuring that all colleagues are treated with respect; ensuring that any confidential information shared in the course of professional communication is also treated confidentially and with respect; obtaining consultation from colleagues when it is appropriate and necessary to serve the clients' best interests; recognizing colleagues' expertise and referring clients to colleagues when it would result in a client being better served; avoiding, as a supervisor, any sexual relations with and/or sexual harassment of any colleague under supervisory authority, including students and trainees, as well as formal employees; and ensuring that any unethical conduct by colleagues is corrected, discouraged, or prevented or else exposed.

Practice Settings Responsibilities

Social worker ethical responsibilities in practice settings include: accepting supervisor or educator duties only if properly qualified; avoiding multiple relationships with students and supervisees; ensuring proper documentation in client records; billing accurately and only for services rendered; advocating for clients that lack adequate resources and/or services; and ensuring that continuing education is available and that staff development is provided to all staff.

Professional Responsibilities

Professional ethical responsibilities include: possessing or promptly pursuing the necessary skills for any employment or assignment accepted; ensuring continuing proficiency in professional practice via ongoing education and learning; avoiding all discrimination against any individuals and groups; ensuring that professional practice is not encumbered by personal problems and issues; and avoiding any solicitation of vulnerable individuals to become clients.

Social workers have ethical responsibilities due to their profession, including: ensuring that high practice standards are maintained and promoted; sustaining, promoting, and preserving the profession's mission, ethics, knowledge, and values; pursuing and promoting research and evaluation that will contribute to the development and knowledge of the profession; and examining and following the programs and policies in social work practice to ensure that they not only are effective but also properly promote the aims and mission of social work.

Social work ethical responsibilities to society include: ensuring that the profession promotes society's general welfare, pursuing equal access to all resources by all individuals through relevant social and political activities, and facilitating social and cultural diversity by supporting and promoting conditions receptive to these special concerns.

HIV Confidentiality Issues

The duty to protect as derived from the *Tarasoff* case has been rigorously debated in terms of other mechanisms of harm—for example, how to handle a situation where a client is HIV positive and is known to be having unprotected sex with a victim who is not aware of the client's HIV-positive status. Given the deadly nature of the sexually and blood-to-blood transmitted human immunodeficiency virus, it has been determined that a social worker or other clinician may be warranted in breaching confidentiality if education about the dangers and efforts at counseling have failed to alter the HIV-positive client's behavior. However, the following five specific criteria must be met: The client must be known to be HIV positive. The client must be engaging in unprotected sex or sharing drug injection paraphernalia. The behavior must actually be unsafe. The client must indicate intent to continue the behavior even after counseling regarding potential harm. HIV transmission must be likely to occur.

Malpractice and Vicarious Liability

A client may allege and sue on grounds of malpractice at any time he or she deems that unprofessional conduct or improper treatment has occurred. In a solo practice, the social worker bears the brunt of this action alone. In an agency setting, liability extends downward from the board of directors to the agency direction to the relevant supervisor, and then to the practicing social worker. Because the costs of such litigation may be high, most agencies carry malpractice insurance, though it can be prudent for agency social workers to carry their own independent policies.

Vicarious liability (also called "imputed negligence" and "respondeat superior") refers to the liability of administrators and supervisors for the actions of those they oversee. If a social worker's conduct is within the scope of employment (even if acting away from the agency) the employer is primarily responsible (though personal liability may still accrue). To this end, supervisors and administrators must be familiar with the case loads and expertise of those they supervise.

Right to Privacy

Every individual has a right to expect that personal information disclosed in a clinical setting, including data such as their address, telephone number, Social Security number, financial information, and health information will not be disclosed to others, and no preconditions need be fulfilled to claim this right. The 1974 Federal Privacy Act (PL 93-579) also stipulates that clients be informed: when records about them are being maintained, that they can access, correct, and copy these records, and that the records are to be used only for the purpose of obtaining absent written consent otherwise. Exceptions are: need-to-know sharing with other agency employees, use for research if identifying information is omitted, release to the government for law enforcement purposes, responding to a subpoena, and in emergencies, where the health and safety of an individual is at risk. While the law applies only to agencies receiving federal funds, many state and local entities have adopted these standards.

Privacy Protection

In 1996 the federal government passed legislation providing privacy protection for personal health information. Known as the Health Insurance Portability and Accountability Act (HIPAA), this act: places privacy protections on personal health information and specifically limits the purposes for its use and the circumstances for its disclosure; provides individuals with specific rights to access their records; and ensures that individuals will be notified about privacy practices. The act applies only to "covered entities," which are defined as health care providers (physicians and allied health care providers), clearinghouses for health care services, and health plans.

The National Association of Social Workers (NASW) has issued a policy on confidentiality. It provides general guidelines, including a client's right to be told of records being maintained and verification of the records for accuracy. It does not, however, specify how individuals may access these records.

Confidentiality

All social workers, supervisors, administrators, clerical and administrative staff, volunteers, and trainees privy to client information are bound by rules of confidentiality.
Confidentiality exceptions include: subpoena, but information released should be only as specifically ordered, arguments regarding relevance and scope may be

useful, and a claim of "privileged communication" may be upheld, depending upon the case; treatment continuity, where vacation or leave by the practitioner, illness coverage, etc., may require other staff to view a client's file or to discuss the case; insurance coverage, which typically requires release of the DSM-IV-TR diagnosis and certain information regarding treatment progress, and the treatment contract the client signs should stipulate this, for liability purposes; client request of release of information to any third party, if by written request; mandated reporting, as previously addressed; and child welfare, where information regarding abuse, harming of self or others, and legal violations must be disclosed to a parent or guardian, and the child should be told this at the outset of the relationship.

Supervision in Social Work

Agency Bureaucratic Levels and Supervisor Responsibilities

An agency typically has three levels of bureaucratic staff: institution-wide leaders, management-level staff, and direct service providers. A supervisor is a "middle manager," overseeing direct service staff and reporting to administrative directors. As a manager, a supervisor provides indirect client services (through front-line staff) and serves primarily the agency. Supervisory roles include: recruitment and orientation, management: delegating duties, overseeing staff work, and resolving conflicts, education, training, and staff development: instructing staff regarding policies and procedures, and ensuring that training is available or pursued via in-service meetings, workshops, and continuing education courses; assessment and review: evaluating and providing feedback regarding staff performance; support: helping staff resolve issues and cope with stress and promoting a healthy work environment; advocacy: resolving complaints and pursuing necessary support for staff; role-modeling of quality practice, values, and ethics; and program evaluator: ensuring that policies and procedures are effective and that staff adhere to guidelines.

Agency Relationships

While all agency staff is concerned with providing quality services, administrators have a more external focus, while supervisors and direct service staff are focused internally. Administrators are charged with broad program planning, policy development, and ensuring agency funding, along with managing the agency's public image and community perceptions. By contrast, supervisors are more responsible for the implementation of policy and programs and ensuring staff adherence to those guidelines provided. New employees (during a "probationary period") and those seeking licensure may engage in more formal supervision experiences. In the case of supervision for licensure, a written agreement will outline the goals, purpose, and scope of the supervision, along with meeting frequency and duration (to accrue required licensure hours), evaluations, whether or not sessions will be recorded (videotaped, etc.), and how feedback will be provided. Consultation and supervision differ, as consultation is an episodic, voluntary problem-solving process with someone having special expertise, in contrast to continuous and mandatory oversight with administrative authority.

Supervisor Ethical Obligations

The NASW Code of Ethics addresses the ethical obligations of supervisors to their employees. Specifically: Social work supervisors should supervise and/or consult within only their area of expertise, knowledge, and competence. Supervisors are responsible for setting proper boundaries that are clear, culturally sensitive, and ethically sound. Social work supervisors should not accept multiple relationships with supervisees where potential harm, exploitation, or other untoward outcome could result (e.g., formalized personal counseling outside the scope of employment). All supervisee evaluations should be provided in a manner that is both fair and respectful.

Practice Evaluation & Utilization of Research

Research

Research is the process by which a hypothesis is either supported or rejected. A hypothesis is a statement of supposition either for or against a specific idea. Standardized processes of data collection explore the hypothesis in a valid, reliable, and replicable way. Research is either qualitative or quantitative. Qualitative research is descriptive and explores an issue, group, or individual. It is inductive and relies largely on focus groups, in-depth interviews, and reviews. It tends to be unstructured, subjective, and nonstatistical and addresses a problem or condition from the perspective experience. Because it is unstructured, the findings tend to be less generalizable to other groups or situations. It is often the first step in the formulation of a theory, preparatory to subsequent quantitative research. Quantitative research is deductive and relies on systematic data collection and analysis, using tools such as objective comparisons, measurements, experiments, and surveys. Because of the formalized, representative, and objective nature of quantitative research, the findings tend to be generalizable.

Research Process and Study Design

The key steps in the research process are: problem or issue identification, including a literature review to ensure that the problem has not already been studied; hypothesis formulation: creating a clear statement of the problem or concern, worded in a way that it can be operationalized and measured; operationalization: creating measurable variables that fully address the hypothesis; and study design selection: choosing a study design that will allow for the proper analysis of the data to be collected.

Key factors guiding the selection of a study design include: standardization: whether or not data can be collected in an identical way from each participant (eliminating collection variation); level of certainty: the study size needed to achieve statistical significance (determined via "power calculations"); resources: the availability of funding and other resources needed; the time frame required; and the capacity of subjects to provide informed consent and ethics approval via Human Subjects Review Committees and Institutional Review Boards.

Common Study Designs

There are three common study designs: exploratory, descriptive, and experimental. An exploratory research design is common when little is known about a particular problem or issue. Its key feature is flexibility. The results comprise detailed descriptions of all observations made, arranged in some kind of order. Conclusions drawn include educated guesses or hypotheses.

When the variables you choose have already been studied (e.g., in an exploratory study), further research requires a descriptive survey design. In this design, the variables are controlled partly by the situation and partly by the investigator, who chooses the sample. Proof of causality cannot be established, but the evidence may support causality.

Experimental studies are highly controlled. Intervening and extraneous variables are eliminated, and independent variables are manipulated to measure effects in dependent variables (e.g., variables of interest)—either in the field or in a laboratory setting.

Data and findings are stored securely to protect confidentiality and prevent tampering.

Single System Design

Evaluation of the efficacy and functionality of a practice is an important aspect of quality control and practice improvement. The most common approach to such an evaluation is the single system study approach. Selecting one client per system ($n = 1$), observations are made prior to, during, and following an intervention. The research steps are: selection of a problem for change (the "target"); operationalizing the target (i.e., into measurable terms); following the target during the "baseline phase" (i.e., prior to the application of any intervention); and observing the target and collecting data during the "intervention phase" (during which the intervention is carried out). There may be more than one phase of data collection. Data that are repeatedly collected constitute a single system study "time series design." Single system designs provide a flexible and efficient way to evaluate virtually any type of practice.

Predesigns

Three types of case study or predesigns are: *Design A*, an observational design with no intervention; *Design B*, an intervention-only design without any baseline; *Design B-C*, a "changes case study" design (where no baseline is recorded, a first intervention ["B"] is performed and then changed ["C"] and data are recorded). The most basic single system design is the "A-B design." The baseline phase ("A") has no intervention, followed by the intervention phase ("B") with data collection. Typically, data are collected continuously through the intervention phase. Advantages of this design include: versatility; adaptability to many settings, program styles, and problems; and clear comparative information between phases. A significant limitation, however, is that causation cannot be demonstrated.

Experimental Single System Designs

The A-B-A design begins with data collection in the pre-intervention phase (A) and then continuously during the intervention phases (B). The intervention is then removed (returning to "A") and data are again collected. In this way an experimental process is produced (testing without, with, and then again without intervention). In this way, inferences regarding causality can be made, and two points of comparison are achieved. However, the ethics of removing a successful intervention leaves this study poorly recommended. The A-B-A-B study overcomes this failure by reintroducing the intervention ("B") at the close of the study. Greater causality inferences are obtained. However, even temporary removal of a successful intervention is problematic (especially if the client drops out at that time), and this design is fairly time-consuming. Therefore, the B-A-B design (the "intervention repeat design") drops the baseline phase and starts and ends with the intervention (important in crisis situations and where treatment delays are problematic), saving time and reducing ethical concerns.

Data Collection

Key points in data collection include: Data should ideally be collected close to the time of intervention (delays may result in variation from forgetfulness, rather than from the intervention process). Frequent data collection is ideal, but subject boredom or fatigue must be avoided as well. Thus, make the data collection process as easy as possible (electronic devices can sometimes help). Keep the data collection process short to increase subject responsiveness. Standardize recording procedures (collect data at the same time, place, and method to enhance ultimate data validity and reliability). Choose a collection method that fits the study well (observation, questionnaires, logs, diaries, surveys, rating scales, etc.) to optimize the data collection process and enhance the value of the data obtained.

Data Analysis

In testing a hypothesis (the assertion that two variables are related), researchers look for correlations between variables (a change in one variable associated with a change in another, expressed in numerical values). The closer the correlation is to +1.0 or –1.0 (a perfect positive or negative correlation), the more meaningful the correlation. This, however, is not causality (change in one variable responsible for change in the other). Since all possible relationships between two variables cannot be tested (the variety approaches infinity), the "null hypothesis" is used (asserting that no relationship exists) with probability statistics that indicate the likelihood that the hypothesis is "null" (and must be rejected) or can be accepted. Indices of "reliability" and "validity" are also needed. Reliability refers to consistency of results (via test–retest evaluations, split-half testing [random assignment into two subgroups given the same intervention and then comparison of findings], or in interrater situations, where separate subjects' rating scores are compared to see if the correlations persist).

Validity

Validity indicates the degree to which a study's results capture the actual characteristics of the features being measured. Reliable results may be consistent but invalid. However, valid results will always be reliable. Methods for testing validity include: *concurrent validity*: comparing the results of studies that used different measurement instruments but targeted the same features; *construct validity*: the degree of agreement between a theoretical concept and the measurements obtained (as seen via the subcategories of "convergent validity," the degree of actual agreement on measures that should be theoretically related, and "discriminant validity," the lack of a relationship among measures which are theoretically not related); *content validity*, comprising "logical validity" (i.e., whether reasoning indicates it is valid) and "*face validity*" (i.e., whether those involved concur that it appears valid); and *predictive validity*, concerning whether the measurement can be used to accurately extrapolate (predict) future outcomes.

Measurement and Sampling

The four different categories of measurement are: nominal: used when two or more "named" variables exist (male/female, pass/fail, etc.); ordinal: used when a hierarchy is present but when the distance between each value is not necessarily equal (e.g., first, second, third place); interval: hierarchal values that are at equal distance from each other; and ratio: one value divided by another, providing a relative association of one quantity in terms of the other (e.g., 50 is one half of 100).

In sampling, a "population" is the total set of subjects sought for measurement by a researcher. A "sample" is a subset of subjects drawn from a population (as total population testing is usually not possible). A "subject" is a single unit of a population. "Generalizability" refers to the degree to which specific findings obtained can be applied to the total population.

Sampling Techniques

Simple random sampling: any method of sampling wherein each subject selected from a population has an equal chance of being selected (e.g., drawing names from a hat). *Stratified random* sampling: dividing a population into desired groups (age, income, etc.) and then using a simple random sample from each stratified group. *Cluster sampling*: a technique used when natural groups are readily evident in a population (e.g., residents within each county in a state). The natural groups are then subjected to random sampling to obtain random members from each county. The best results occur when elements within clusters are internally heterogeneous and externally (between clusters) homogeneous, as the formation of natural clusters may introduce error and bias.

Systematic sampling: a systematic method of random sampling (e.g., randomly choosing a number *n* between 1 and 10—perhaps drawing the number from a hat) and then selecting every *n*th name in the phone book to obtain a study sample.

Measures of Variability

"Measures of variability" (or variation) include: the "range," which is the arithmetic difference between the largest and the smallest value (idiosyncratic "outliers" often excluded); the "interquartile range," which is the difference between the upper and lower quartiles (e.g., between the 75th and 25th percentiles); and the "standard deviation," which is the average distance that numerical values are dispersed around the arithmetic mean. "Correlation" refers to the strength of relatedness when a relationship exists between two or more numerical values, which, when assigned a numerical value, is the "correlation coefficient" (*r*). A perfect (1:1) correlation has an *r* value of 1.0, with decimal values indicating a lesser correlation as the correlation coefficient moves away from 1.0. The correlation may be either positive (with the values increasing or decreasing together) or negative (if the values are inverse and move opposite to each other).

Statistical Test

A "statistical test" seeks to prove something by means of contradiction (e.g., via a failure to reject a null hypothesis). There are five key components: a "research hypothesis" (HA): declaring what you intend to prove; a "null hypothesis" (HO): a statement declaring that no relationship, meaning, or value change exists; a "test statistic" (TS): the computed value which indicates whether or not to reject the null hypothesis in favor of the research hypothesis, or to retain the null hypothesis; the "rejection region" (RR): a range or computational region wherein results between those values must be rejected; and the "conclusion": a summary statement indicating whether the research hypothesis was accepted or rejected.

Statistical tests presume the null hypothesis to be true and use the values derived from a test to calculate the likelihood of getting the same or better results under the conditions of the null hypothesis (referred to as the "observed probability" or "empirical probability," as opposed to the "theoretical probability"). Where this likelihood is very small, the null hypothesis is rejected. Traditionally, experimenters have defined a "small chance" at the 0.05 level (sometimes called the 5% level) or the 0.01 level (1% level). The Greek letter alpha (α) is used to indicate the significance level chosen. Where the observed or empirical probability is less than or equal to the selected alpha, the findings are said to be "statistically significant," and the research hypothesis would be accepted. Types of statistical error are: Type I error: rejecting the null hypothesis when it is true; Type II error: accepting the null hypothesis when it is false and the research hypothesis is true (concluding that a difference, or "beta," doesn't exist when it does).

Statistical Significant Tests

Three examples of tests of statistical significance are: the *"chi square" test* (a "nonparametric" test of significance), which assesses whether or not two samples are sufficiently different to conclude that the difference can be generalized to the larger population from which the samples were drawn. It provides the "degree of confidence" by which the research hypothesis can be accepted or rejected (measured on a scale from zero [impossibility] to one [certainty]); a "t-test," used to compare the arithmetic means of a given characteristic in two samples and to determine whether they are sufficiently different from each other to be statistically significant; and *analysis of variance*, or "ANOVA" (also called the or "*F* test"), which is similar to the *t*-test. However, rather than simply comparing the means of two populations, it is used to determine whether or not statistically significant differences exist in multiple groups or samples.

Terms

A "statistic" is a numerical representation of an identified characteristic of a subject. "Descriptive statistics" are mathematically derived values that represent characteristics identified in a group or population. "Inferential statistics" are mathematical calculations that produce generalizations about a group or population from the numerical values of known characteristics. "Measures of central tendency" identify the relative degree to which certain characteristics in a population are grouped together. Such measures include the "mean," which is the arithmetic average, the "median," which is the numerical value above which 50% of the population is found and below which the other 50% is located, the "mode," which is the most frequently appearing value (score) in a series of numerical values.

Service Delivery

Social Services

Social services endeavor to maintain quality of life in society and include social welfare (poverty and poor health prevention via "entitlements"), along with other government and privately operated programs, services, and resources. Types of social services include: education, employment, health and medical services, housing, minimum income grants, nutrition, retirement, and welfare (for children and the elderly).

Benefits include cash grants (e.g., unemployment, supplemental income) and "in kind" benefits (e.g., food stamps). Delivery systems include:

- employment-based, obtained by or through employment (health insurance, retirement, and disability [both short and long term, including maternity and family leave])
- government-based, consisting of tax relief, such as deductions (e.g., dependents, medical costs) at the local, state, or federal level
- philanthropy-based, comprising programs for needy families, at-risk youth, etc.
- personal contributions, such as child care, private health care, etc.
- public-based, whereby not-for-profit agencies and public agencies provide services, such as shelters, adoption services, and disaster relief, free or at a reduced rate (sliding scale, etc.).

Government Funding

Government programs are funded by income taxes and Social Security taxes. Income taxes are termed "progressive" because they increase as income increases. Taxes such as sales taxes and Social Security taxes are termed "regressive" because they are "flat rate" taxes that offer nonproportional relief to those in low-income situations. Flat-rate tax reform efforts have continued to fall short primarily because of the loss of available deductions, in spite of proposals for tax elimination for the very poor. Dependent deductions can be crucial to low-income families, and home mortgage deductions are crucial for some homebuyers. A trend to "privatization" of government programs has been noted in recent years (e.g., government oversight and funding of privately operated agencies). However, concerns about adequacy, availability, and accountability remain concerning.

Eligibility Criteria and SSA

Eligibility for social services can be determined in many different ways. Three common methods include: universal eligibility: open to all applicants; selective eligibility: specific criteria (age, dependent children, etc.) and often "means tested" (for income and resources) with sliding scale costs; and exceptional eligibility: open only to individuals or groups with special needs (e.g., veterans, people with specific disabilities) and usually not means tested.

The Social Security Act (SSA) of 1935 provided "old age survivor" benefits, with full coverage at age 65. Full eligibility gradually increases to age 67 for those born in or after 1960. To be fully "vested," one must have 40 lifetime credits (earned at 4 credits per year). Reduced compensation may be available for those retiring earlier. Today, the program covers not only retirees, but those with certain permanent disabilities and the minor children of deceased beneficiaries, in certain situations. As an "insurance trust fund," the program was intended to be self-sustaining by all those who pay in.

SSD, Worker's Compensation, and SSI

Individuals with a permanent disability severe enough to prevent them from becoming gainfully employed may qualify for Social Security Disability (SSD). The disabling condition must be expected to last for at least one year or to result in the individual's demise. Individuals who contract a job-related illness or who are injured in the course of their work are covered by the social insurance program known as Worker's Compensation. Injuries resulting from intoxication, gross negligence, or deliberate misconduct are not covered. Coverage varies from state to state for this federally mandated state-administered program. Funding is primarily employer based, though some states may supplement operation costs. Supplemental Security Income (SSI) is a federally funded program supplemented by the state. It ensures a baseline cash income to bring means-tested recipients above the poverty line. Poor elderly, disabled, and blind persons are the primary recipients.

Medicare

Medicare was established in 1965 and is now run by the Centers for Medicare and Medicaid Services. Coverage was initially instituted solely for those over age 65 but was expanded in 1973 to include the disabled (including those with end-stage renal disease). Eligibility criteria include an individual/spouse having worked for at least 10 years in Medicare-covered employment, and U.S. citizenship. Coverage may include up to four "parts": Part A: hospital insurance (hospital care, skilled nursing home care, hospice, and home health care); Part B: medical insurance (doctor's services and outpatient hospital services, diagnostic tests, ambulance transport, some preventive care including mammography and Pap tests, and durable medical equipment and supplies); Part C: Medicare Advantage (MA), run by private companies to provide Part A and Part B benefits and, often, additional benefits such as vision, hearing, and health and wellness programs; Part D: Medicare Advantage–Prescription Drug plans (MA-PD) that include prescription drug coverage.

Food and Nutrition Assistance Programs

Multiple food and nutrition assistance programs exist: *Food Stamps*: coupons to purchase approved groceries, issued according to family size and income (selective eligibility, means-tested), state-administered and federally funded; *WIC* (Women, Infants, and Children): a means-tested, selective eligibility program providing assistance to pregnant women, mothers of infants up to 5 months old, breastfeeding mothers of infants up to 12 months old, and children under age 5 years. Subsidies are provided for specific nutritious foods (infant formula, eggs, etc.). The program is state administered and federally funded; *school lunch programs*: federally funded assistance to children in means-tested families; the *Elderly Nutrition Program*: food assistance for needy persons over age 60 via local churches and community centers; and *Meals on Wheels*: delivery of meals to means-tested individuals and families via this locally funded and administered program.

TANF and General Assistance

The Temporary Assistance for Needy Families (TANF) program replaced the Aid to Families with Dependent Children (AFDC) program. TANF was created by the 1996 Personal Responsibility and Work Opportunity Reconciliation Act and is a federally funded, state-administered block grant program. The focus is on moving recipients into the workforce and returning welfare to its intended temporary and transitional role. General Assistance (GA) refers to a variety of social welfare programs developed by state and local government to aid those unable to meet eligibility for federal assistance programs. Eligibility criteria vary from state to state (even region to region, in some areas). Because there is no mandate for GA programs, they do not exist in all states, though most states have created some form of safety net of this kind.

Housing and Health Care Programs

Public housing consists of government-built residential facilities that provide low-cost to no-cost rent for means-tested poor individuals and families. The Subsidized Housing Program offers federal funds to reduce rental costs for the means-tested poor and to aid in maintaining public residential facilities. Additional public housing assistance programs include home loan assistance programs, home maintenance assistance programs, and "Section 8" low-income reduced rent programs.

Medical assistance for the means-tested poor is covered primarily by the Medicaid program (Medi-Cal, in California). Jointly funded by federal and state funds, the program was created in 1965 under Title XIX of the Social Security Act. The federal government imposes certain guidelines, around which the states establish eligibility standards, services, and rates, and provide overall administration. Medicaid is generally limited to means-tested families with children, recipients of SSI, foster care and adoption assistance recipients, infants born to women receiving Medicaid, children younger than age 6, and pregnant women in families living at or below 133% of the national poverty line.

Unemployment Insurance and Child Welfare

Unemployment insurance is a benefit to prevent undue economic hardship, providing for individuals who become involuntarily and temporarily unemployed. To be eligible, an individual must be actively seeking gainful employment. Benefits include job-seeking assistance and cash payments in reduced proportion to the lost income. The benefits are time limited and once exhausted they cannot be obtained again unless a new episode of employment and job loss occurs. Originating with the Social Security Act of 1935, the program is federally mandated and state administered. Funding comes from employer taxes, distributed by the states to those needing assistance.

A variety of child welfare services and programs have been created for the safety, care, and support of abused, disabled, homeless, and otherwise vulnerable children. Services include adoption and foster care. Agencies investigating abuse and securing out-of-home placement, if necessary, also exist, along with programs for family maintenance and reunification.

Social Service Client Rights

Fundamental client rights in social work services include:

- confidentiality and privacy
- informed consent
- access to services (if service requirements cannot be met, a referral should be offered)
- access to records (adequately protective but not onerously burdensome policies for client access to services should be developed and put in place)
- participation in the development of treatment plans (client cooperation in the treatment process is essential to success)
- options for alternative services/referrals (clients should always be offered options whenever they are available)
- right to refuse services (clients have a right to refuse services that are not court ordered; ethical issues exist when involuntary treatment is provided, but mandates do not allow options other than referrals to other sources of the mandated service)
- termination by the client (clients have a right to terminate services at any time and for any reason they deem adequate, except in certain court-ordered situations).

Social Work Administration

Agency Overview

All organizations should have a "mission statement," setting forth the purpose, goals, and target service population of the organization. An organizational structure is then needed to pursue the delivery of services and achievement of the identified goals.

Typical social service agencies follow a classic Weberian bureaucratic model of organization. In a bureaucracy, leadership flows from the "top down," and tasks are rationally delegated to employees and departments best suited to achieve administrative and agency goals. Key characteristics of a bureaucracy include: labor divided by functions and tasks according to specialized skills or a specific focus needed, a hierarchical structure of authority, recruitment and hiring based upon an initial review of key qualifications and technical skills, rigid rules and procedures generally applied impartially throughout the organization and specifying employee benefits, duties, and rights, and activities and responsibilities that are rationally planned to achieve overarching agency goals.

Administrator Role

Basic administrative functions include: human resource management: recruiting, interviewing, hiring, and firing, as well as orienting and reassigning employees within the organization; planning and delegation: ensuring that the organization's mission, goals, objectives, and policies are in place, appropriate, and effective, and delegating necessary tasks to achieve these ends; employee evaluations, reviews, and monitoring to ensure competency and efficiency; advocacy: horizontal interventions (between staff or across a department) and vertical interventions (between departments and hierarchical staff relationships to resolve conflicts and complaints; and conflict resolution: acting as a mediator and a protector of the various parties involved, ensuring equitable outcomes that remain within the scope of the organization and its goals.

Not-For-Profit Agencies

Not-for-profit (nonprofit) entities operate, in many ways, similar to for-profit entities. However, there are some key differences: Not-for-profit organizations must not be structured to pursue commercial purposes (i.e., profiteering on goods and services sold to the public). Members of a not-for-profit organization may not personally benefit as shareholders or investors. Certain tax benefits can accrue to not-for-profit organizations, within parameters defined by the Internal Revenue Service, which are not available to for-profit entities. Finally, the goals of these organizations tend to be charitable in nature (e.g., caring for vulnerable populations), and they seek and receive funding primarily via government and philanthropic grants, as well as from gifts, donations, and fundraising events.

Administrator Code of Ethics

The Code of Ethics is as applicable to administrators as to primary service providers. Specifically: maintaining the pertinence of advocacy for clients' needs, applied at the intra- and interagency level of planning and resource allocation; ensuring that resource and service allocations are based on consistent principles and are not discriminatory in any way; making sure that proper supervision is available for necessary staff oversight; ensuring that the NASW Code of Ethics is supported and applied in the work setting, and removing any barriers to full compliance that may exist; and providing or arranging for the provision of continuing education and staff development and ensuring staff release time for these purposes.

Boards of Directors

The power and authority vested in a board of directors depends upon whether they are overseeing a private or public agency. Public agencies have board members that are largely advisory or administrative, with less direct authority than those overseeing private entities. In private agencies or voluntary organizations, the board is empowered to define the general path of the agency and to control all systems and programs operating under its auspices. The board is responsible to any sources that provide monetary contributions, to the community, to the government, and to all consumers that use the agency's programs. To be successful, members of a social service agency's board must have knowledge of all operations. The function of the board is to oversee the design of policies, develop short- and long-term planning, confirm the hiring of personnel, oversee general finances and financial expenditures, deal with the public, and be accountable for the actions of the agency.

The agency's mission and overall goals must be kept paramount when choosing board members. Members must be committed, honest, and able to invest their time and energy in the agency. Responsibilities must be discharged with personal expertise and through meaningful relationships within the community. Interpersonal skills are essential, as board members deal directly with the other members of the board, professionals at the agency, and the general public. Some boards require the representation of certain professions within the community (e.g., a banker), but all members must bring a particular expertise to the board. The agency's mission and the personal responsibilities of each board member should be understood, and a specific orientation experience should be provided to ensure this understanding. Terms are typically limited to three years, with the possibility of a second term for those making unique contributions. The terms should rotate to ensure that seasoned board members are always available.

Linking and Monitoring

Case managers must link clients with the service providers and resources needed, to the extent appropriate resources are available. Case managers are also responsible for helping clients overcome any obstacles in using the resources they are provided. When a client is unable to articulate his or her own needs, case managers must advocate and speak for them to get the assistance required. If necessary, help from an agency's administrative staff may be needed to fully address the services required. High-quality continuous monitoring is a key case management function. Good working relationships between case managers, clients, and direct service providers are essential to ensure a successful monitoring and accommodation process. Changes in plans and linkages may at times become necessary, as the client and/or available services may change and evolve.

Case Consultation

Case consultation involves communication between a social worker and a direct service provider. The client could be an individual, family, or community. To be successful, consultation must have a purpose, a problem, and a process. The person requesting the consultation has the right to decline help, so the consultant must have high-value ideas to gain the trust of the consultee. An effective consultation process requires that the consultee determine the need for consultation and initiate the request for consultation, while the consultant and consultee must collaborate in assessing the problem, determine a plan for help, negotiate contracts, have a mutual list of objectives, determine the action to be taken, implement the plan, and measure and report the outcomes in a clear and concise manner. Communication is at the core of the process, so the consultant must have quality communication and problem-solving skills to be successful.

Sample Test Questions

1. In treating a client in crisis, the caseworker should focus on
    a. the immediate presenting problem
    b. a few specific problems in day-to-day functioning
    c. a wide range of problems in day-to-day functioning
    d. underlying personality problems

2. A social worker is interviewing a new patient who presents some symptoms of depression. The patient reports recent changes such as diminished functioning, marked weight gain, early morning awakening, fatigue, inability to concentrate, suicidal thoughts and headaches. The patient mentions that he started a new medication for a medical condition three weeks ago. The worker would first:
    a. arrange a psychiatric consultation in order to have an anti-depressant prescribed
    b. ascertain the prescribed medication and investigate its side-effects
    c. proceed with a thorough psychosocial history and precipitating events
    d. hospitalize this patient until the suicidal ideation passes

3. A social worker is utilizing environmental manipulation as a technique when he/she:
    a. represents the agency at a health and welfare council meeting
    b. uses a psychosocial framework
    c. suggests the use of psychoactive medications
    d. helps the client find more satisfying employment in a supportive environment

4. A diagnosis of Schizophreniform Disorder is generally applied to clients whose psychotic symptoms:
    a. are related to substance abuse
    b. are very long term
    c. show a marked and continuing decline in functioning
    d. are similar to those of schizophrenia and have existed more than one month, but less than six months.

5. A 15-year-old female patient at a mental health clinic complains that for the past three weeks she has been uncharacteristically angry and irritable and has had difficulty concentrating on school work. She says that she feels "down in the dumps". Her appetite has diminished and though weighing 120 pounds a month earlier, she has lost 9 pounds. She has difficulty sleeping and has withdrawn from after school activities that she had previously found interesting and enjoyable. During the interview she seems constantly in motion, rising several times and walking around the room before returning to her chair. It is most likely that she is suffering from:
   a. a drug induced depression
   b. a somatoform disorder
   c. a depressive episode
   d. an adolescent behavior disorder

6. The policy of providing Permanency Planning refers to:
   a. children who are at risk of removal or are removed from their own homes
   b. the development of a plan through which abused and neglected children will be assured of a stable family situation throughout childhood
   c. a stable foster care plan for children removed from their homes
   d. the use of adoption for children at risk

7. DSM permits certain diagnoses for mental disorders to be made, even though the diagnosis does not totally fit DSM criterion. These diagnoses are normally modified by the word:
   a. revised
   b. provisional
   c. temporary
   d. latent

8. A social worker and his agency supervisor are sued for malpractice by the family of a teen age boy who made several attempts at suicide and finally succeeded in killing himself. Which statement best reflects the supervisor's legal status in this lawsuit?

    a. Since the supervisor was not the direct clinician and had never personally treated the youth, she is not liable for any negligent actions committed by others in the agency.

    b. The supervisor shares vicarious legal liability and is responsible for carefully monitoring and evaluating the status of every case under treatment by her supervisees, and for keeping records concerning the supervisee's work on the case.

    c. The agency is the only legally liable party and the workers are not individually responsible.

    d. In cases such as these, parents often believe that a finding of negligence on the part of the clinician will reduce their sense of loss and failure. The lawsuit is probably frivolous and neither the worker, nor the supervisor is responsible.

9. A patient presents at an ambulatory care facility and is in obvious psychological distress, showing severe anxiety and paranoia. The clinician is unable to determine the exact configuration of the patient's symptoms, but is certain that it is an Anxiety Disorder. The worker is unable to determine if the is order is primary, caused by the patient's severe kidney disease or related to other factors such as the patient's continuing substance abuse. The most likely DSM diagnosis is;

    a. Anxiety Disorder, with generalized anxiety

    b. Anxiety Disorder, undifferentiated

    c. Anxiety Disorder, NOS

    d. Anxiety Disorder, provisional

10. A school social worker interviews a 15 year old male student with an IQ of 70. Though assigned to slower classes, the student maintains social relationships and is able to respond appropriately to teachers and class mates. His school work is within the range that would be expected for his recorded IQ. He can read somewhat below grade level and is able to do very basic arithmetic. He is also able to follow instructions and is generally amiable in responding to coaching and correction. In developing a plan with this student and the family, the social worker would:

    a. plan for eventual supervised residence in a facility for the mentally disabled

    b. establish a plan that includes vocational preparation and that will eventually lead to independent living.

    c. emphasize vocational achievement in the near term

    d. provide coaching and tutoring to improve his reading

11. A DSM diagnosis of a specific disorder generally includes a criterion of:
   a. a clinically significant impairment, or distress in a social, occupational, or other important area.
   b. a description that includes an identifiable etiology
   c. distress that exceeds 6 weeks
   d. no medical involvement

12. A DSM diagnosis:
   a. provides sufficient information for developing a treatment plan
   b. ends the treatment planning process
   c. is insufficient by itself for treatment planning
   d. is an early or intermediate step in the treatment planning process.

13. A DSM diagnosis often includes a specifier or suffix to delineate the severity of the disorder. The usual specifier is:
   a. mild, moderate or severe,
   b. in partial remission
   c. in full remission
   d. prior history

14. A client begins treatment with a social worker and tells the social worker that he must promise never to involuntarily hospitalize him no matter how depressed or suicidal he may seem. The underlying ethical principle that determines the social worker's response is:
   a. The obligation to start where the client is
   b. The expectation that the client has good reasons to raise this issue.
   c. The need to do what is necessary to keep a severely ill client from ending treatment.
   d. Never to make a promise that is in conflict with legal and ethical requirements.

15. A social worker who attempts to impose her judgments on clients is most likely to elicit clients':
   a. acquiescence
   b. cooperation
   c. resistance
   d. appreciation

16. In a first interview, a worker observes that the client moves slowly, with stooped posture, talks slowly and in a lifeless way, lacks spontaneity, and shows little change in facial expression as they discuss the client's problem.
The worker would most likely suspect:
    a. depression
    b. a manic stage
    c. anxiety
    d. delusional thinking

17. In a first session at an HMO mental health clinic with a couple who want to address marital problems, the wife complains that the biggest problem in their marriage is the husband's nasty temper. The worker's best response is:
    a. can you tell me more about this problem?
    b. have you done anything that might provoke his anger?
    c. at our session today he doesn't seem to have a problem with self control.
    d. to ask the husband if he wishes to discuss his problems with his temper

18. A social worker at a health center is working with a young adolescent group concerned with drug and alcohol prevention. The social worker is uneasy about conflicts within the group and is fearful that they may interfere with group process. The worker's supervisor might initially:
    a. seek to delineate and resolve the worker's personal history with regard to conflict
    b. communicate support, indicating that controversy and conflict may be normal and natural means for resolving issues
    c. inquire about the concerns of the worker and reflect back the issues without resolving them
    d. suggest that the worker not reach any conclusions and bring in any issues which might arise

19. Children who suffer physical, mental or emotional injuries inflicted by caretaking adults are commonly termed:
    a. children of poverty
    b. abused or neglected children
    c. developmentally masochistic
    d. victims

20. Under most state laws, mental health professionals must alert child welfare agencies or other lawful authorities to:
    a. suspicion of child abuse
    b. evidence of child sexual abuse
    c. imminent threats to a child
    d. child custody battles

21. A supervisor wants to observe a supervisee's client interview through a two way mirror. Because the supervisor is a professional staff member with overall responsibility for all cases in treatment by staff, the worker would:
a. not need to obtain the client's informed consent since the observation's purpose is supervision
b. not have to obtain informed consent of the client, since such consent is given when clients sign a release form for information at intake
c. have to obtain the client's informed consent on the observation and its use
d. have to obtain informed consent only if the session is to be recorded

22. A social worker is conducting a small counseling group. The members seem to have some difficulty in beginning. A statement the worker would not make is:
a. In what way can I help you to begin?
b. Who might like to begin?
c. It's sometimes difficult to begin
d. It seems hard to begin today

23. A hospital patient is referred to social services after she complains of insufficient money for food. After talking with the patient, the worker's diagnosis is that the patient, although from a low income family, is not indigent. She seems to consistently have difficulties managing money and does not appear to handle her funds appropriately. Her diet appears nutritionally adequate. The worker's most suitable action would be to:
a. help the patient obtain assistance from a casework agency for help with money management
b. provide continuing casework treatment through the hospital social service department to insure that her diet remains adequate
c. suggest to the patient that she apply to the public welfare agency to determine eligibility for public assistance
d. reassure the patient that her income can be made to cover her essential needs

24. A social worker using a psychosocial casework approach is not likely to:
a. consider the client-worker relationship to be a basic therapeutic tool
b. rely on psychiatric diagnostic-classifications
c. be concerned with the client's interaction with the environment
d. frequently use novel, unconventional treatments

25. The process of assessment is the task of the:
a. social worker
b. client
c. social worker and the client
d. agency psychiatrist

Answer Key

1. The correct answer is (a).
The immediate presenting problem as it is perceived by the client is the only possible arena in which a social worker can intervene. Other responses will be perceived by the client as non-responsive to his or her concerns.

2. The correct answer is (b).
Medications can have powerful side effects and should be ruled out as a causative factor. 1. a psychiatric consultation is unnecessary at this time 2. the clients current mental state and inability to concentrate suggest that a psychosocial history will not be feasible.

3. The correct answer is (d).
Environmental manipulation suggests the employment of specific changes in the client's life that will improve their immediate situation.

4. The correct answer is (d).

5. The correct answer is (c).
The only other possible answer is 1, however drug use is not mentioned as a factor in the girl's life and no history of drug use is cited.

6. The correct answer is (b).
It is the most general answer and describes the broad outlines of the policy's intention in regard to children at risk.

7. The correct answer is (b).
This is a fact question and is unambiguous.

8. The correct answer is (b).
A supervisor is legally responsible for cases under supervision and shares personal responsibility with the supervisee. The agency is also liable since their agents performed the actions leading to the alleged damage.

9. The correct answer is (c).
This is a fact question. NOS is an abbreviation for Not Otherwise Specified.

10. The correct answer is (b).
The youth's functioning seems appropriate for his IQ and his achievement are within normal range. The question refers to the development of a plan and the answer should reflect a planning response. Given the youth's age and high

functioning, it is likely that he can eventually find employment and live independently. This should be a focus of the social worker.

11. The correct answer is (a).
This is a fact question and refers to specific criteria of DSM-IV-TR.

12. The correct answer is (d).
1 is incorrect since DSM is descriptive. 2. Is incorrect as treatment planning is dynamic and continues throughout treatment. 3. does not account for the need for narrative that captures the tone and attitude of family members. A DSM diagnosis is ordinarily an early step in the diagnostic phase of work with the client and is normally an early stage of treatment planning.

13. The correct answer is (a).
This is a fact question and is based on information found in the DSM.

14. The correct answer is (d).
Answer 1 refers to a practice principle not an ethical principle. Answer 2 is irrelevant and 3 would seem opportunistic and manipulative. The social worker's obligation is to be honest and make his or her professional obligations clear to the client.

15. The correct answer is (c).
Resistance usually occurs when a practitioner attempts to impose a judgment that a client is not prepared to accept.

16. The correct answer is (a).
No other response fits the constellation of factors described in the question.

17. The correct answer is (a).
It is the only response that is responsive to the wife's statement.

18. The correct answer is (b).
In this question, the correct response is the one that emphasizes the supervisor's educational function, while reassuring the worker that conflict is a part of group process. Answer 1. - helping the worker deal with his or her own issues regarding conflict alters the supervisory relationship and tilts it into a therapeutic situation. Answers 3 and 4 do not help the worker with the immediate problem.

19. The correct answer is (b).
The stem of the question is a common definition of child abuse.

20. The correct answer is (a).
A good faith child abuse report requires only that the worker suspect that abuse has occurred. Evidence (response #2) is a much higher standard and is not required for a report.

21. The correct answer is (c).
When third parties are viewing sessions it is ethically imperative that the client is aware of the situation. Even if they have previously signed a release, the worker is required to let the client know when actual observations are taking place.

22. The correct answer is (a).
The other three responses place the responsibility on the group to find a way to begin interacting. Answer number one places the responsibility on the worker and suggests that it is the worker's obligation to take charge. The worker's role is to encourage and reflect to the group.

23. The correct answer is (a).
After identifying money management as the primary problem, the best strategy is to provide help for the problem. The other three responses are not germane to the client's presenting problem. She neither needs public assistance or assistance with nutrition issues since she has an adequate diet.

24. The correct answer is (d).
All of the issues described in responses 1-3 are part of the psychosocial approach. Novel or untested approaches would not be used without the permission of the client.

25. The correct answer is (c).
Assessment is a shared responsibility of client and social worker. It is also a pragmatic approach to achieving client cooperation in working on the identified problems.

Secret Key #1 - Time is Your Greatest Enemy

Pace Yourself

Wear a watch. At the beginning of the test, check the time (or start a chronometer on your watch to count the minutes), and check the time after every few questions to make sure you are "on schedule."

If you are forced to speed up, do it efficiently. Usually one or more answer choices can be eliminated without too much difficulty. Above all, don't panic. Don't speed up and just begin guessing at random choices. By pacing yourself, and continually monitoring your progress against your watch, you will always know exactly how far ahead or behind you are with your available time. If you find that you are one minute behind on the test, don't skip one question without spending any time on it, just to catch back up. Take 15 fewer seconds on the next four questions, and after four questions you'll have caught back up. Once you catch back up, you can continue working each problem at your normal pace.

Furthermore, don't dwell on the problems that you were rushed on. If a problem was taking up too much time and you made a hurried guess, it must be difficult. The difficult questions are the ones you are most likely to miss anyway, so it isn't a big loss. It is better to end with more time than you need than to run out of time.

Lastly, sometimes it is beneficial to slow down if you are constantly getting ahead of time. You are always more likely to catch a careless mistake by working more slowly than quickly, and among very high-scoring test takers (those who are likely to have lots of time left over), careless errors affect the score more than mastery of material.

Secret Key #2 - Guessing is not Guesswork

You probably know that guessing is a good idea - unlike other standardized tests, there is no penalty for getting a wrong answer. Even if you have no idea about a question, you still have a 20-25% chance of getting it right.

Most test takers do not understand the impact that proper guessing can have on their score. Unless you score extremely high, guessing will significantly contribute to your final score.

Monkeys Take the Test

What most test takers don't realize is that to insure that 20-25% chance, you have to guess randomly. If you put 20 monkeys in a room to take this test, assuming they answered once per question and behaved themselves, on average they would get 20-25% of the questions correct. Put 20 test takers in the room, and the average will be much lower among guessed questions. Why?

1. The test writers intentionally write deceptive answer choices that "look" right. A test taker has no idea about a question, so picks the "best looking" answer, which is often wrong. The monkey has no idea what looks good and what doesn't, so will consistently be lucky about 20-25% of the time.

2. Test takers will eliminate answer choices from the guessing pool based on a hunch or intuition. Simple but correct answers often get excluded, leaving a 0% chance of being correct. The monkey has no clue, and often gets lucky with the best choice.

This is why the process of elimination endorsed by most test courses is flawed and detrimental to your performance- test takers don't guess, they make an ignorant stab in the dark that is usually worse than random.

$5 Challenge

Let me introduce one of the most valuable ideas of this course- the $5 challenge:

You only mark your "best guess" if you are willing to bet $5 on it.
You only eliminate choices from guessing if you are willing to bet $5 on it.

Why $5? Five dollars is an amount of money that is small yet not insignificant, and can really add up fast (20 questions could cost you $100). Likewise, each answer choice on one question of the test will have a small impact on your overall score, but it can really add up to a lot of points in the end.

The process of elimination IS valuable. The following shows your chance of guessing it right:

If you eliminate wrong answer choices until only this many answer choices remain:	1	2	3
Chance of getting it correct:	100%	50%	33%

However, if you accidentally eliminate the right answer or go on a hunch for an incorrect answer, your chances drop dramatically: to 0%. By guessing among all the answer choices, you are GUARANTEED to have a shot at the right answer.

That's why the $5 test is so valuable- if you give up the advantage and safety of a pure guess, it had better be worth the risk.

What we still haven't covered is how to be sure that whatever guess you make is truly random. Here's the easiest way:

Always pick the first answer choice among those remaining.

Such a technique means that you have decided, **before you see a single test question**, exactly how you are going to guess- and since the order of choices tells you nothing about which one is correct, this guessing technique is perfectly random.

This section is not meant to scare you away from making educated guesses or eliminating choices- you just need to define when a choice is worth eliminating. The $5 test, along with a pre-defined random guessing strategy, is the best way to make sure you reap all of the benefits of guessing.

Secret Key #3 - Practice Smarter, Not Harder

Many test takers delay the test preparation process because they dread the awful amounts of practice time they think necessary to succeed on the test. We have refined an effective method that will take you only a fraction of the time.

There are a number of "obstacles" in your way to succeed. Among these are answering questions, finishing in time, and mastering test-taking strategies. All must be executed on the day of the test at peak performance, or your score will suffer. The test is a mental marathon that has a large impact on your future.

Just like a marathon runner, it is important to work your way up to the full challenge. So first you just worry about questions, and then time, and finally strategy:

Success Strategy

1.   Find a good source for practice tests.
2.   If you are willing to make a larger time investment, consider using more than one study guide- often the different approaches of multiple authors will help you "get" difficult concepts.
3.   Take a practice test with no time constraints, with all study helps "open book." Take your time with questions and focus on applying strategies.
4.   Take a practice test with time constraints, with all guides "open book."
5.   Take a final practice test with no open material and time limits

If you have time to take more practice tests, just repeat step 5. By gradually exposing yourself to the full rigors of the test environment, you will condition your mind to the stress of test day and maximize your success.

Secret Key #4 - Prepare, Don't Procrastinate

Let me state an obvious fact: if you take the test three times, you will get three different scores. This is due to the way you feel on test day, the level of preparedness you have, and, despite the test writers' claims to the contrary, some tests WILL be easier for you than others.

Since your future depends so much on your score, you should maximize your chances of success. In order to maximize the likelihood of success, you've got to prepare in advance. This means taking practice tests and spending time learning the information and test taking strategies you will need to succeed.

Never take the test as a "practice" test, expecting that you can just take it again if you need to. Feel free to take sample tests on your own, but when you go to take the official test, be prepared, be focused, and do your best the first time!

Secret Key #5 - Test Yourself

Everyone knows that time is money. There is no need to spend too much of your time or too little of your time preparing for the test. You should only spend as much of your precious time preparing as is necessary for you to get the score you need.

Once you have taken a practice test under real conditions of time constraints, then you will know if you are ready for the test or not.

If you have scored extremely high the first time that you take the practice test, then there is not much point in spending countless hours studying. You are already there.

Benchmark your abilities by retaking practice tests and seeing how much you have improved. Once you score high enough to guarantee success, then you are ready.

If you have scored well below where you need, then knuckle down and begin studying in earnest. Check your improvement regularly through the use of practice tests under real conditions. Above all, don't worry, panic, or give up. The key is perseverance!

Then, when you go to take the test, remain confident and remember how well you did on the practice tests. If you can score high enough on a practice test, then you can do the same on the real thing.

General Strategies

The most important thing you can do is to ignore your fears and jump into the test immediately- do not be overwhelmed by any strange-sounding terms. You have to jump into the test like jumping into a pool- all at once is the easiest way.

Make Predictions

As you read and understand the question, try to guess what the answer will be. Remember that several of the answer choices are wrong, and once you begin reading them, your mind will immediately become cluttered with answer choices designed to throw you off. Your mind is typically the most focused immediately after you have read the question and digested its contents. If you can, try to predict what the correct answer will be. You may be surprised at what you can predict.

Quickly scan the choices and see if your prediction is in the listed answer choices. If it is, then you can be quite confident that you have the right answer. It still won't hurt to check the other answer choices, but most of the time, you've got it!

Answer the Question

It may seem obvious to only pick answer choices that answer the question, but the test writers can create some excellent answer choices that are wrong. Don't pick an answer just because it sounds right, or you believe it to be true. It MUST answer the question. Once you've made your selection, always go back and check it against the question and make sure that you didn't misread the question, and the answer choice does answer the question posed.

Benchmark

After you read the first answer choice, decide if you think it sounds correct or not. If it doesn't, move on to the next answer choice. If it does, mentally mark that answer choice. This doesn't mean that you've definitely selected it as your answer choice, it just means that it's the best you've seen thus far. Go ahead and read the next choice. If the next choice is worse than the one you've already selected, keep going to the next answer choice. If the next choice is better than the choice you've already selected, mentally mark the new answer choice as your best guess.

The first answer choice that you select becomes your standard. Every other answer choice must be benchmarked against that standard. That choice is correct until proven otherwise by another answer choice beating it out. Once you've decided that no other answer choice seems as good, do one final check to ensure that your answer choice answers the question posed.

Valid Information

Don't discount any of the information provided in the question. Every piece of information may be necessary to determine the correct answer. None of the information in the question is there to throw you off (while the answer choices will certainly have information to throw you off). If two seemingly unrelated topics are discussed, don't ignore either. You can be confident there is a relationship, or it wouldn't be included in the question, and you are probably going to have to determine what is that relationship to find the answer.

Avoid "Fact Traps"

Don't get distracted by a choice that is factually true. Your search is for the answer that answers the question. Stay focused and don't fall for an answer that is true but incorrect. Always go back to the question and make sure you're choosing an answer that actually answers the question and is not just a true statement. An answer can be factually correct, but it MUST answer the question asked. Additionally, two answers can both be seemingly correct, so be sure to read all of the answer choices, and make sure that you get the one that BEST answers the question.

Milk the Question

Some of the questions may throw you completely off. They might deal with a subject you have not been exposed to, or one that you haven't reviewed in years. While your lack of knowledge about the subject will be a hindrance, the question itself can give you many clues that will help you find the correct answer. Read the question carefully and look for clues. Watch particularly for adjectives and nouns describing difficult terms or words that you don't recognize. Regardless of if you completely understand a word or not, replacing it with a synonym either provided or one you more familiar with may help you to understand what the questions are asking. Rather than wracking your mind about specific detailed information concerning a difficult term or word, try to use mental substitutes that are easier to understand.

The Trap of Familiarity

Don't just choose a word because you recognize it. On difficult questions, you may not recognize a number of words in the answer choices. The test writers don't put "make-believe" words on the test; so don't think that just because you only recognize all the words in one answer choice means that answer choice must be correct. If you only recognize words in one answer choice, then focus on that one. Is it correct? Try your best to determine if it is correct. If it is, that is great, but if it doesn't, eliminate it. Each word and answer choice you eliminate increases your chances of getting the question correct, even if you then have to guess among the unfamiliar choices.

Eliminate Answers

Eliminate choices as soon as you realize they are wrong. But be careful! Make sure you consider all of the possible answer choices. Just because one appears right, doesn't mean that the next one won't be even better! The test writers will usually put more than one good answer choice for every question, so read all of them. Don't worry if you are stuck between two that seem right. By getting down to just two remaining possible choices, your odds are now 50/50. Rather than wasting too much time, play the odds. You are guessing, but guessing wisely, because you've been able to knock out some of the answer choices that you know are wrong. If you are eliminating choices and realize that the last answer choice you are left with is also obviously wrong, don't panic. Start over and consider each choice again. There may easily be something that you missed the first time and will realize on the second pass.

Tough Questions

If you are stumped on a problem or it appears too hard or too difficult, don't waste time. Move on! Remember though, if you can quickly check for obviously incorrect answer choices, your chances of guessing correctly are greatly improved. Before you completely give up, at least try to knock out a couple of possible answers. Eliminate what you can and then guess at the remaining answer choices before moving on.

Brainstorm

If you get stuck on a difficult question, spend a few seconds quickly brainstorming. Run through the complete list of possible answer choices. Look at each choice and ask yourself, "Could this answer the question satisfactorily?" Go through each answer choice and consider it independently of the other. By systematically going through all possibilities, you may find something that you would otherwise overlook. Remember that when you get stuck, it's important to try to keep moving.

Read Carefully

Understand the problem. Read the question and answer choices carefully. Don't miss the question because you misread the terms. You have plenty of time to read each question thoroughly and make sure you understand what is being asked. Yet a happy medium must be attained, so don't waste too much time. You must read carefully, but efficiently.

Face Value

When in doubt, use common sense. Always accept the situation in the problem at face value. Don't read too much into it. These problems will not require you to make huge leaps of logic. The test writers aren't trying to throw you off with a cheap trick. If you have to go beyond creativity and make a leap of logic in order to have an answer choice answer the question, then you should look at the other answer choices. Don't overcomplicate the problem by creating theoretical relationships or explanations that will warp time or space. These are normal problems rooted in reality. It's just that the applicable relationship or explanation may not be readily apparent and you have to figure things out. Use your common sense to interpret anything that isn't clear.

Prefixes

If you're having trouble with a word in the question or answer choices, try dissecting it. Take advantage of every clue that the word might include. Prefixes and suffixes can be a huge help. Usually they allow you to determine a basic meaning. Pre- means before, post- means after, pro - is positive, de- is negative. From these prefixes and suffixes, you can get an idea of the general meaning of the word and try to put it into context. Beware though of any traps. Just because con is the opposite of pro, doesn't necessarily mean congress is the opposite of progress!

Hedge Phrases

Watch out for critical "hedge" phrases, such as likely, may, can, will often, sometimes, often, almost, mostly, usually, generally, rarely, sometimes. Question writers insert these hedge phrases to cover every possibility. Often an answer choice will be wrong simply because it leaves no room for exception. Avoid answer choices that have definitive words like "exactly," and "always".

Switchback Words

Stay alert for "switchbacks". These are the words and phrases frequently used to alert you to shifts in thought. The most common switchback word is "but". Others include although, however, nevertheless, on the other hand, even though, while, in spite of, despite, regardless of.

New Information

Correct answer choices will rarely have completely new information included. Answer choices typically are straightforward reflections of the material asked about and will directly relate to the question. If a new piece of information is included in an answer choice that doesn't even seem to relate to the topic being asked about, then that answer choice is likely incorrect. All of the information needed to answer the question is usually provided for you, and so you should not have to make guesses that are unsupported or choose answer choices that require unknown information that cannot be reasoned on its own.

Time Management

On technical questions, don't get lost on the technical terms. Don't spend too much time on any one question. If you don't know what a term means, then since you don't have a dictionary, odds are you aren't going to get much further. You should immediately recognize terms as whether or not you know them. If you don't, work with the other clues that you have, the other answer choices and terms provided, but don't waste too much time trying to figure out a difficult term.

Contextual Clues

Look for contextual clues. An answer can be right but not correct. The contextual clues will help you find the answer that is most right and is correct. Understand the context in which a phrase or statement is made. This will help you make important distinctions.

Don't Panic

Panicking will not answer any questions for you. Therefore, it isn't helpful. When you first see the question, if your mind goes blank, take a deep breath. Force yourself to mechanically go through the steps of solving the problem and using the strategies you've learned.

Pace Yourself

Don't get clock fever. It's easy to be overwhelmed when you're looking at a page full of questions, your mind is full of random thoughts and feeling confused, and the clock is ticking down faster than you would like. Calm down and maintain the pace that you have set for yourself. As long as you are on track by monitoring your pace, you are guaranteed to have enough time for yourself. When you get to the last few minutes of the test, it may seem like you won't have enough time left, but if you only have as many questions as you should have left at that point, then you're right on track!

Answer Selection

The best way to pick an answer choice is to eliminate all of those that are wrong, until only one is left and confirm that is the correct answer. Sometimes though, an answer choice may immediately look right. Be careful! Take a second to make sure that the other choices are not equally obvious. Don't make a hasty mistake. There are only two times that you should stop before checking other answers. First is when you are positive that the answer choice you have selected is correct. Second is when time is almost out and you have to make a quick guess!

Check Your Work

Since you will probably not know every term listed and the answer to every question, it is important that you get credit for the ones that you do know. Don't miss any questions through careless mistakes. If at all possible, try to take a second to look back over your answer selection and make sure you've selected the correct

- 124 -

answer choice and haven't made a costly careless mistake (such as marking an answer choice that you didn't mean to mark). This quick double check should more than pay for itself in caught mistakes for the time it costs.

Beware of Directly Quoted Answers

Sometimes an answer choice will repeat word for word a portion of the question or reference section. However, beware of such exact duplication – it may be a trap! More than likely, the correct choice will paraphrase or summarize a point, rather than being exactly the same wording.

Slang

Scientific sounding answers are better than slang ones. An answer choice that begins "To compare the outcomes..." is much more likely to be correct than one that begins "Because some people insisted..."

Extreme Statements

Avoid wild answers that throw out highly controversial ideas that are proclaimed as established fact. An answer choice that states the "process should be used in certain situations, if..." is much more likely to be correct than one that states the "process should be discontinued completely." The first is a calm rational statement and doesn't even make a definitive, uncompromising stance, using a hedge word "if" to provide wiggle room, whereas the second choice is a radical idea and far more extreme.

Answer Choice Families

When you have two or more answer choices that are direct opposites or parallels, one of them is usually the correct answer. For instance, if one answer choice states "x increases" and another answer choice states "x decreases" or "y increases," then those two or three answer choices are very similar in construction and fall into the same family of answer choices. A family of answer choices is when two or three answer choices are very similar in construction, and yet often have a directly opposite meaning.   Usually the correct answer choice will be in that family of answer choices. The "odd man out" or answer choice that doesn't seem to fit the parallel construction of the other answer choices is more likely to be incorrect.

Special Report: How to Overcome Test Anxiety

The very nature of tests caters to some level of anxiety, nervousness or tension, just as we feel for any important event that occurs in our lives. A little bit of anxiety or nervousness can be a good thing. It helps us with motivation, and makes achievement just that much sweeter. However, too much anxiety can be a problem; especially if it hinders our ability to function and perform.

"Test anxiety," is the term that refers to the emotional reactions that some test-takers experience when faced with a test or exam. Having a fear of testing and exams is based upon a rational fear, since the test-taker's performance can shape the course of an academic career. Nevertheless, experiencing excessive fear of examinations will only interfere with the test-takers ability to perform, and his/her chances to be successful.

There are a large variety of causes that can contribute to the development and sensation of test anxiety. These include, but are not limited to lack of performance and worrying about issues surrounding the test.

Lack of Preparation

Lack of preparation can be identified by the following behaviors or situations:

Not scheduling enough time to study, and therefore cramming the night before the test or exam

Managing time poorly, to create the sensation that there is not enough time to do everything

Failing to organize the text information in advance, so that the study material consists of the entire text and not simply the pertinent information

Poor overall studying habits

Worrying, on the other hand, can be related to both the test taker, or many other factors around him/her that will be affected by the results of the test. These include worrying about:

Previous performances on similar exams, or exams in general

How friends and other students are achieving

The negative consequences that will result from a poor grade or failure

There are three primary elements to test anxiety. Physical components, which involve the same typical bodily reactions as those to acute anxiety (to be discussed below). Emotional factors have to do with fear or panic. Mental or cognitive issues concerning attention spans and memory abilities.

Physical Signals

There are many different symptoms of test anxiety, and these are not limited to mental and emotional strain. Frequently there are a range of physical signals that will let a test taker know that he/she is suffering from test anxiety. These bodily changes can include the following:

Perspiring

Sweaty palms

Wet, trembling hands

Nausea

Dry mouth

A knot in the stomach

Headache

Faintness

Muscle tension

Aching shoulders, back and neck

Rapid heart beat

Feeling too hot/cold

To recognize the sensation of test anxiety, a test-taker should monitor him/herself for the following sensations:

The physical distress symptoms as listed above

Emotional sensitivity, expressing emotional feelings such as the need to cry or laugh too much, or a sensation of anger or helplessness

A decreased ability to think, causing the test-taker to blank out or have racing thoughts that are hard to organize or control.

Though most students will feel some level of anxiety when faced with a test or exam, the majority can cope with that anxiety and maintain it at a manageable level. However, those who cannot are faced with a very real and very serious condition, which can and should be controlled for the immeasurable benefit of this sufferer.

Naturally, these sensations lead to negative results for the testing experience. The most common effects of test anxiety have to do with nervousness and mental blocking.

Nervousness

Nervousness can appear in several different levels:

The test-taker's difficulty, or even inability to read and understand the questions on the test

The difficulty or inability to organize thoughts to a coherent form

The difficulty or inability to recall key words and concepts relating to the testing questions (especially essays)

The receipt of poor grades on a test, though the test material was well known by the test taker

Conversely, a person may also experience mental blocking, which involves:

Blanking out on test questions

Only remembering the correct answers to the questions when the test has already finished.

Fortunately for test anxiety sufferers, beating these feelings, to a large degree, has to do with proper preparation. When a test taker has a feeling of preparedness, then anxiety will be dramatically lessened.

The first step to resolving anxiety issues is to distinguish which of the two types of anxiety are being suffered. If the anxiety is a direct result of a lack of preparation, this should be considered a normal reaction, and the anxiety level (as opposed to the test results) shouldn't be anything to worry about. However, if, when adequately prepared, the test-taker still panics, blanks out, or seems to overreact, this is not a fully rational reaction. While this can be considered normal too, there are many ways to combat and overcome these effects.

Remember that anxiety cannot be entirely eliminated, however, there are ways to minimize it, to make the anxiety easier to manage. Preparation is one of the best ways to minimize test anxiety. Therefore the following techniques are wise in order to best fight off any anxiety that may want to build.

To begin with, try to avoid cramming before a test, whenever it is possible. By trying to memorize an entire term's worth of information in one day, you'll be shocking your system, and not giving yourself a very good chance to absorb the information. This is an easy path to anxiety, so for those who suffer from test anxiety, cramming should not even be considered an option.

Instead of cramming, work throughout the semester to combine all of the material which is presented throughout the semester, and work on it gradually as the course goes by, making sure to master the main concepts first, leaving minor details for a week or so before the test.

To study for the upcoming exam, be sure to pose questions that may be on the examination, to gauge the ability to answer them by integrating the ideas from your texts, notes and lectures, as well as any supplementary readings.

If it is truly impossible to cover all of the information that was covered in that particular term, concentrate on the most important portions, that can be covered very well. Learn these concepts as best as possible, so that when the test comes, a goal can be made to use these concepts as presentations of your knowledge.

In addition to study habits, changes in attitude are critical to beating a struggle with test anxiety. In fact, an improvement of the perspective over the entire test-taking experience can actually help a test taker to enjoy studying and therefore improve the overall experience. Be certain not to overemphasize the significance of the grade - know that the result of the test is neither a reflection of self worth, nor is it a measure of intelligence; one grade will not predict a person's future success.

To improve an overall testing outlook, the following steps should be tried:

Keeping in mind that the most reasonable expectation for taking a test is to expect to try to demonstrate as much of what you know as you possibly can.
Reminding ourselves that a test is only one test; this is not the only one, and there will be others.
The thought of thinking of oneself in an irrational, all-or-nothing term should be avoided at all costs.
A reward should be designated for after the test, so there's something to look forward to. Whether it be going to a movie, going out to eat, or simply visiting friends, schedule it in advance, and do it no matter what result is expected on the exam.

Test-takers should also keep in mind that the basics are some of the most important things, even beyond anti-anxiety techniques and studying. Never neglect the basic social, emotional and biological needs, in order to try to absorb information. In order to best achieve, these three factors must be held as just as important as the studying itself.

Study Steps

Remember the following important steps for studying:

Maintain healthy nutrition and exercise habits. Continue both your recreational activities and social pass times. These both contribute to your physical and emotional well being.

Be certain to get a good amount of sleep, especially the night before the test, because when you're overtired you are not able to perform to the best of your best ability. Keep the studying pace to a moderate level by taking breaks when they are needed, and varying the work whenever possible, to keep the mind fresh instead of getting bored.

When enough studying has been done that all the material that can be learned has been learned, and the test taker is prepared for the test, stop studying and do something relaxing such as listening to music, watching a movie, or taking a warm bubble bath.

There are also many other techniques to minimize the uneasiness or apprehension that is experienced along with test anxiety before, during, or even after the examination. In fact, there are a great deal of things that can be done to stop anxiety from interfering with lifestyle and performance. Again, remember that anxiety will not be eliminated entirely, and it shouldn't be. Otherwise that "up" feeling for exams would not exist, and most of us depend on that sensation to perform better than usual. However, this anxiety has to be at a level that is manageable.

Of course, as we have just discussed, being prepared for the exam is half the battle right away. Attending all classes, finding out what knowledge will be expected on the exam, and knowing the exam schedules are easy steps to lowering anxiety. Keeping up with work will remove the need to cram, and efficient study habits will eliminate wasted time. Studying should be done in an ideal location for concentration, so that it is simple to become interested in the material and give it complete attention. A method such as SQ3R (Survey, Question, Read, Recite, Review) is a wonderful key to follow to make sure that the study habits are as effective as possible, especially in the case of learning from a textbook. Flashcards are great techniques for memorization. Learning to take good notes will mean that notes will be full of useful information, so that less sifting will need to be done to seek out what is pertinent for studying. Reviewing notes after class and then again on occasion will keep the information fresh in the mind. From notes that have been taken summary sheets and outlines can be made for simpler reviewing.

A study group can also be a very motivational and helpful place to study, as there will be a sharing of ideas, all of the minds can work together, to make sure that everyone understands, and the studying will be made more interesting because it will be a social occasion.

Basically, though, as long as the test-taker remains organized and self confident, with efficient study habits, less time will need to be spent studying, and higher grades will be achieved.

To become self confident, there are many useful steps. The first of these is "self talk." It has been shown through extensive research, that self-talk for students who suffer from test anxiety, should be well monitored, in order to make sure that it contributes to self confidence as opposed to sinking the student. Frequently the self talk of test-anxious students is negative or self-defeating, thinking that everyone else is smarter and faster, that they always mess up, and that if they don't do well, they'll fail the entire course. It is important to decreasing anxiety that awareness is made of self talk. Try writing any negative self thoughts and then disputing them with a positive statement instead. Begin self-encouragement as though it was a friend speaking. Repeat positive statements to help reprogram the mind to believing in successes instead of failures.

Helpful Techniques

Other extremely helpful techniques include:

Self-visualization of doing well and reaching goals

While aiming for an "A" level of understanding, don't try to "overprotect" by setting your expectations lower. This will only convince the mind to stop studying in order to meet the lower expectations.

Don't make comparisons with the results or habits of other students. These are individual factors, and different things work for different people, causing different results.

Strive to become an expert in learning what works well, and what can be done in order to improve. Consider collecting this data in a journal.

Create rewards for after studying instead of doing things before studying that will only turn into avoidance behaviors.

Make a practice of relaxing - by using methods such as progressive relaxation, self-hypnosis, guided imagery, etc - in order to make relaxation an automatic sensation.

Work on creating a state of relaxed concentration so that concentrating will take on the focus of the mind, so that none will be wasted on worrying.

Take good care of the physical self by eating well and getting enough sleep.

Plan in time for exercise and stick to this plan.

Beyond these techniques, there are other methods to be used before, during and after the test that will help the test-taker perform well in addition to overcoming anxiety.

Before the exam comes the academic preparation. This involves establishing a study schedule and beginning at least one week before the actual date of the test. By doing this, the anxiety of not having enough time to study for the test will be automatically eliminated. Moreover, this will make the studying a much more effective experience, ensuring that the learning will be an easier process. This relieves much undue pressure on the test-taker.

Summary sheets, note cards, and flash cards with the main concepts and examples of these main concepts should be prepared in advance of the actual studying time. A topic should never be eliminated from this process. By omitting a topic because it isn't expected to be on the test is only setting up the test-taker for anxiety should it actually appear on the exam. Utilize the course syllabus for laying out the topics that should be studied. Carefully go over the notes that were made in class, paying special attention to any of the issues that the professor took special care to emphasize while lecturing in class. In the textbooks, use the chapter review, or if possible, the chapter tests, to begin your review.

It may even be possible to ask the instructor what information will be covered on the exam, or what the format of the exam will be (for example, multiple choice, essay, free form, true-false). Additionally, see if it is possible to find out how many questions will be on the test. If a review sheet or sample test has been offered by the professor, make good use of it, above anything else, for the preparation for the test. Another great resource for getting to know the examination is reviewing tests from previous semesters. Use these tests to review, and aim to achieve a 100% score on each of the possible topics. With a few exceptions, the goal that you set for yourself is the highest one that you will reach.

Take all of the questions that were assigned as homework, and rework them to any other possible course material. The more problems reworked, the more skill and confidence will form as a result. When forming the solution to a problem, write out each of the steps. Don't simply do head work. By doing as many steps on paper as possible, much clarification and therefore confidence will be formed. Do this with as many homework problems as possible, before checking the answers. By checking the answer after each problem, a reinforcement will exist, that will not be on the exam. Study situations should be as exam-like as possible, to prime the test-taker's system for the experience. By waiting to check the answers at the end, a psychological advantage will be formed, to decrease the stress factor.

Another fantastic reason for not cramming is the avoidance of confusion in concepts, especially when it comes to mathematics. 8-10 hours of study will become one hundred percent more effective if it is spread out over a week or at least several days, instead of doing it all in one sitting. Recognize that the human brain requires time in order to assimilate new material, so frequent breaks and a span of study time over several days will be much more beneficial.

Additionally, don't study right up until the point of the exam. Studying should stop a minimum of one hour before the exam begins. This allows the brain to rest and put things in their proper order. This will also provide the time to become as relaxed as possible when going into the examination room. The test-taker will also have time to eat well and eat sensibly. Know that the brain needs food as much as the rest of the body. With enough food and enough sleep, as well as a relaxed attitude, the body and the mind are primed for success.

Avoid any anxious classmates who are talking about the exam. These students only spread anxiety, and are not worth sharing the anxious sentimentalities.

Before the test also involves creating a positive attitude, so mental preparation should also be a point of concentration. There are many keys to creating a positive attitude. Should fears become rushing in, make a visualization of taking the exam, doing well, and seeing an A written on the paper. Write out a list of affirmations that will bring a feeling of confidence, such as "I am doing well in my English class," "I studied well and know my material," "I enjoy this class." Even if the affirmations aren't believed at first, it sends a positive message to the subconscious which will result in an alteration of the overall belief system, which is the system that creates reality.

If a sensation of panic begins, work with the fear and imagine the very worst! Work through the entire scenario of not passing the test, failing the entire course, and dropping out of school, followed by not getting a job, and pushing a shopping cart through the dark alley where you'll live. This will place things into perspective! Then, practice deep breathing and create a visualization of the opposite situation - achieving an "A" on the exam, passing the entire course, receiving the degree at a graduation ceremony.

On the day of the test, there are many things to be done to ensure the best results, as well as the most calm outlook. The following stages are suggested in order to maximize test-taking potential:

Begin the examination day with a moderate breakfast, and avoid any coffee or beverages with caffeine if the test taker is prone to jitters. Even people who are used to managing caffeine can feel jittery or light-headed when it is taken on a test day.

Attempt to do something that is relaxing before the examination begins. As last minute cramming clouds the mastering of overall concepts, it is better to use this time to create a calming outlook.

Be certain to arrive at the test location well in advance, in order to provide time to select a location that is away from doors, windows and other distractions, as well as giving enough time to relax before the test begins.

Keep away from anxiety generating classmates who will upset the sensation of stability and relaxation that is being attempted before the exam.

Should the waiting period before the exam begins cause anxiety, create a self-distraction by reading a light magazine or something else that is relaxing and simple.

During the exam itself, read the entire exam from beginning to end, and find out how much time should be allotted to each individual problem. Once writing the exam, should more time be taken for a problem, it should be abandoned, in order to begin another problem. If there is time at the end, the unfinished problem can always be returned to and completed.

Read the instructions very carefully - twice - so that unpleasant surprises won't follow during or after the exam has ended.

When writing the exam, pretend that the situation is actually simply the completion of homework within a library, or at home. This will assist in forming a relaxed atmosphere, and will allow the brain extra focus for the complex thinking function.

Begin the exam with all of the questions with which the most confidence is felt. This will build the confidence level regarding the entire exam and will begin a quality momentum. This will also create encouragement for trying the problems where uncertainty resides.

Going with the "gut instinct" is always the way to go when solving a problem. Second guessing should be avoided at all costs. Have confidence in the ability to do well.

For essay questions, create an outline in advance that will keep the mind organized and make certain that all of the points are remembered. For multiple choice, read every answer, even if the correct one has been spotted - a better one may exist.

Continue at a pace that is reasonable and not rushed, in order to be able to work carefully. Provide enough time to go over the answers at the end, to check for small errors that can be corrected.

Should a feeling of panic begin, breathe deeply, and think of the feeling of the body releasing sand through its pores. Visualize a calm, peaceful place, and include all of the sights, sounds and sensations of this image. Continue the deep breathing, and take a few minutes to continue this with closed eyes. When all is well again, return to the test.

If a "blanking" occurs for a certain question, skip it and move on to the next question. There will be time to return to the other question later. Get everything done that can be done, first, to guarantee all the grades that can be compiled, and to build all of the confidence possible. Then return to the weaker questions to build the marks from there.

Remember, one's own reality can be created, so as long as the belief is there, success will follow. And remember: anxiety can happen later, right now, there's an exam to be written!

After the examination is complete, whether there is a feeling for a good grade or a bad grade, don't dwell on the exam, and be certain to follow through on the reward that was promised...and enjoy it! Don't dwell on any mistakes that have been made, as there is nothing that can be done at this point anyway.

Additionally, don't begin to study for the next test right away. Do something relaxing for a while, and let the mind relax and prepare itself to begin absorbing information again.

From the results of the exam - both the grade and the entire experience, be certain to learn from what has gone on. Perfect studying habits and work some more on confidence in order to make the next examination experience even better than the last one.

Learn to avoid places where openings occurred for laziness, procrastination and day dreaming.

Use the time between this exam and the next one to better learn to relax, even learning to relax on cue, so that any anxiety can be controlled during the next exam. Learn how to relax the body. Slouch in your chair if that helps. Tighten and then relax all of the different muscle groups, one group at a time, beginning with the feet and then working all the way up to the neck and face. This will ultimately relax the muscles more than they were to begin with. Learn how to breathe deeply and comfortably, and focus on this breathing going in and out as a relaxing thought. With every exhale, repeat the word "relax."

As common as test anxiety is, it is very possible to overcome it. Make yourself one of the test-takers who overcome this frustrating hindrance.

Special Report: Additional Bonus Material

Due to our efforts to try to keep this book to a manageable length, we've created a link that will give you access to all of your additional bonus material.

Please visit http://www.mometrix.com/bonus948/swbachelors to access the information.